the Wolves *of* Yellowstone

BY MICHAEL K. PHILLIPS AND DOUGLAS W. SMITH

PHOTOGRAPHS BY BARRY AND TERI O'NEILL

FOREWORD BY JOHN D. VARLEY,
DIRECTOR OF THE YELLOWSTONE CENTER FOR RESOURCES

With reflections on the historic wolf reintroduction by U.S. Interior Secretary Bruce Babbitt; U.S. Fish and Wildlife Service Director Mollie Beattie; wolf researcher L. David Mech; Ed Bangs, Steven Fritts, and Joe Fontaine of the U.S. Fish and Wildlife Service; Yellowstone Superintendent Mike Finley; John D. Varley, Wayne G. Brewster, Norman Bishop, and Paul Schullery of the Yellowstone Center for Resources; Mark R. Johnson of the National Park Service; Carter Niemeyer of the Agriculture Department's Animal Damage Control Program; the Wolf Fund's Renee Askins; Defenders of the Wildlife's Hank Fischer; and *The Billings Gazette*'s cartoonist John Potter

Voyageur Press

Dedication

To my parents, Jack and Patty, and my wife, Linda. Thank you for all you have done.
—Michael K. Phillips

To my mother, Billie E. Smith, who was there when nobody else was.
—Douglas W. Smith

To our children, Ross, Regina, and Sean. This book is for you: May it inspire you to find a way to make this world a better place for your children. All it takes is a dream and the belief that if you can dream it, you can make it happen.
—Barry and Teri O'Neill

Edited by Michael Dregni
Designed by Helene C. J. Anderson
Printed in China

First hardcover edition

| 97 | 98 | 99 | 00 | 5 | 4 | 3 | 2 |

First softcover edition

| 02 | 03 | 04 | 6 | 5 | 4 | 3 |

Library of Congress Cataloging-in-Publication Data
Phillips, Michael K., 1958–
The wolves of Yellowstone / Michael K. Phillips, Douglas W. Smith; photographs by Barry and Teri O'Neill.
p. cm.
Includes bibliographical references (p. 125) and index.
ISBN 0-89658-330-9
ISBN 0-89658-391-0 (pbk.)
1. Wolves—Yellowstone National Park. 2. Wildlife reintroduction—Yellowstone National Park. 3. Yellowstone National Park. 4. Wolves—Yellowstone National Park—Pictorial works. 5. Wildlife reintroduction—Yellowstone National Park—Pictorial works. 6. Yellowstone National Park—Pictorial works. I. Smith, Douglas W. II. Title.
QL737.C22P5 1996
599.74'442—dc20   96–14286
CIP

Distributed in Canada by Raincoast Books, 9050 Shaughnessy Street, Vancouver, B.C. V6P 6E5

Published by Voyageur Press, Inc.
123 North Second Street, P.O. Box 338, Stillwater, MN 55082 U.S.A.
651-430-2210, fax 651-430-2211

Please write or call, or stop by, for our free catalog of natural history publications. Our toll-free number to place an order or to obtain a free catalog is 800-888-WOLF (800-888-9653).
Educators, fundraisers, premium and gift buyers, publicists, and marketing managers: Looking for creative products and new sales ideas? Voyageur Press books are available at special discounts when purchased in quantities, and special editions can be created to your specifications. For details contact the marketing department.

Page 1: *The silver wolf, alpha female #39, from the 1996 batch of wolves in the Rose Creek pen.*

ACKNOWLEDGMENTS

Wolves again roam the forests and valleys of Yellowstone because of tremendous efforts of many people. Make no mistake, it took a true team effort to bring the wolves home. And just as certainly, it will take a true team effort to ensure that the wolves never again disappear.

Countless employees of Yellowstone contributed mightily to the wolf's reintroduction, not only in 1995, but during previous years as well. John Varley, Director of the Yellowstone Center for Resources, worked for a decade to return the wolf to Yellowstone. He continues to be a source of inspiration and guidance. Wayne Brewster, Deputy Director of the Yellowstone Center for Resources, worked for fifteen years on wolf recovery in the Rocky Mountains. Wayne is due a world of credit for wolves roaming freely in Yellowstone and northwestern Montana. Mike Finley, Superintendent of Yellowstone, is an ardent supporter of the restoration effort and did much behind-the-scenes work to ensure the success of the project's first year. Doug and I very much appreciate Mike's efforts and can-do approach to conservation. Wolf restoration is fraught with uncertainty. Doug and I appreciate the trust that Mike, John, and Wayne place in us as we follow our instincts with the many varied aspects of the program. We look forward to working for these men well into the future.

Norm Bishop, research interpreter for the Center for Resources, educated more people about wolves than anyone else in the West. Marsha Karle, Chief of Public Affairs for Yellowstone Park, and her staff did an outstanding job distributing accurate information to the media. Dr. Mark Johnson was responsible for many activities in Yellowstone and also coordinated veterinary support and services for the wolves' Canadian translocation. Park wranglers Bob Blackwell, Ben Cunningham, and Wally Wines did outstanding jobs, as did volunteers Carol Anderson, Debrah Guernsey, Brian Johnson, Dan McNulty, Lessie Redman, Carrie Schaeffer, Dr. J. Douglas Smith, and Nathan Varley.

Other Yellowstone employees deserve mention as well. From the Yellowstone Center for Resources: Mark Biel, Sue Consolo-Murphy, Kerry Gunther, Bob Lindstrom, John Mack, Melissa McAdam, Joy Perius, and Paul Schullery. From the Maintenance Division: Al Bowers, Jim Evanoff, and Betty Cates. From the Ranger Division: Dick Bahr, Brian Chan, Colette Daigle-Berg, Mona Divine, Les Inafuku, Michael Keator, Dave Kreutzer, Mike Murray, Phil Perkins, Bob Seibert, and all the rangers who worked to ensure the welfare of the wolves during acclimation. Countless other employees from all divisions in Yellowstone contributed to the success of the first year. Apologies to all who are not specifically mentioned.

Ed Bangs, Joe Fontaine, and Dr. Steve Fritts of the U.S. Fish and Wildlife Service have been involved in nearly every aspect of the Yellowstone program, and are due more credit than can be written on this page. Carter Niemyer is the Wolf Management Specialist for Animal Damage Control, the federal agency responsible for managing wolf-livestock interactions. Drs. L. David Mech and Rolf O. Peterson probably know more about wolves than any two people on the planet; their counsel proved invaluable. Dave Mech and Paul Schullery also reviewed this book and offered suggestions that improved it greatly. Renee Askins, founder and director of the Wolf Fund, worked tirelessly for years to bring the wolf back to Yellowstone. Hank Fischer and Defenders of Wildlife are due credit for many things, including establishing the depredation compensation fund that helps to ensure that wolves will not become a burden to livestock producers.

Finally, we thank our wives, Linda and Tristen, who contributed in myriad ways.

To these individuals, and to all the people who have helped make this dream a reality, we offer our congratulations on a job well done. Without your efforts there would be no wolves in Yellowstone. You have made a difference, you have righted a wrong, you have set an example for others to follow, you have helped make this world a better place.

Mike Phillips and Doug Smith
Yellowstone National Park
March 1996

Black wolf running through the snow
Alpha male #35 from the 1996 group of wolves runs along the inside perimeter of the Blacktail pen, surveying his new surroundings.

Only the mountain has lived long enough to listen objectively to the howl of a wolf.
—Aldo Leopold, 1949

CONTENTS

Acknowledgments   3

Foreword by John D. Varley   7
DIRECTOR OF THE YELLOWSTONE CENTER FOR RESOURCES

Introduction by Barry O'Neill   9
EXECUTIVE DIRECTOR OF THE CALL OF THE WILD FOUNDATION

Photography Notes   10

CHAPTER 1, Beginnings   13

CHAPTER 2, A Strategy for Restoring Wolves   25

CHAPTER 3, Capture and Translocation   33

CHAPTER 4, The Adventure Begins   45

CHAPTER 5, Acclimation   55

CHAPTER 6, Release   65

CHAPTER 7, Freedom   75

CHAPTER 8, Kills   85

CHAPTER 9, Red Lodge Rescue   93

CHAPTER 10, Incident at Dry Creek   107

CHAPTER 11, Into the Future   117

Suggested Readings   125

Index   126

Haunting eyes
Wolf pup #21 watches the new world from its kennel box. This pup was one of the first litter of wolves to be born in Yellowstone in sixty years, the offspring of wolf #9.

FOREWORD

To those of us in Yellowstone's prime-time seats, the week the first shipment of Canadian wolves arrived, we knew we were watching history—important history at that—being made before our very eyes. That was one feeling among the participants, but it wasn't the most common or even the most intense feeling. But for each person involved in the week of the wolf "coming home," it was an unequivocally and intensely personal experience.

I saw tears in the eyes of others and felt tears myself when the wolf caravan crept through the historic Roosevelt Arch at the north entrance to the park. Some of the wolf team were so pumped up with adrenaline you could feel the voltage. Others, even those most closely involved with the wolf restoration process, could only say, "I can't believe it's actually happening," or "I would have bet a month's pay against this ever happening." I didn't hear of Las Vegas making odds on Yellowstone wolves, but given the nationwide notoriety of the issue, and the fact that 80 percent of the regional populace had a strong opinion pro or con, it would not have surprised me. I could not believe it was happening, either; I kept expecting several of the western senators to have somehow ordered the Air Force to strafe our convoy. But once these magnificent Canadian beasts were inside the park, I also had the feeling wolves had come to Yellowstone to stay.

As Hank Fischer alludes to in his smashing book *Wolf Wars*, the actual arrival of wolves to Yellowstone was, more than anything, a celebration of the end of a great decade-long siege; arguably the greatest battle to date over the control and influence agribusiness has regarding policy on western public lands. With wolves, the agribusiness giants lost a big one, and many thought the same thing we thought: "I can't believe this is actually happening." I suspect they will spend the next decade trying to get the wolves back out of Yellowstone.

The "Year of the Wolf" in Yellowstone was, by anyone's measure, a first-class rollercoaster ride. Our public and press had the notion that everything should have been very predictable—like a high school physics experiment—despite the fact that we told them over and over that it was an experiment that had never been tried before. Our Canadian wolves, however, did not read our recipe book. Early on, they seemed to delight in giving us heart-stopping excursions to places nobody thought they should be, only to be back in "The Lamar" thirty-six hours later. They provided surprise and joy when two of the packs had unexpected litters, and also when it became obvious they thought our elk were good fare to eat. They gave us a share of sadness too, like when #10 was murdered, and when #22—#9 and #10's magnificent pup—was killed by a truck.

Because each of the contributors to this volume had large or small jobs associated with the war itself, or with planning for the actual event, or with the event itself through the first year, I think most of us felt pleased and privileged to be a part of such a precedent-setting happening. At one point, several of us attempted to put together a list of people who had to be thanked for their help in making it all happen, but after entering the 225th name, with no end in sight, we became frustrated because of the sheer scale of the project. Where to start and end such a list? Do names for this list start in 1944 with Aldo Leopold's bold statement about finding wolves a home in Yellowstone? Or does it start a decade before that with yet another visionary, George Wright, and his colleagues? But these people only had a great idea. What about the people who had the vision to really make it happen? The late National Park Service Director William Penn Mott or Yellowstone Superintendent Bob Barbee come to mind as splendid examples. Or what about the fox-hole lieutenants and captains like Wayne Brewster and Ed Bangs who, on a daily basis, took the gut shots and kept standing up for more. Or Mike Phillips and Doug Smith, designated recipients and nurturers of the precious Canadian cargo, who as commanders of the rollercoaster, knew that if they screwed it up, they, too, would be a significant part of history.

But the more I thought about our "thank-you list" dilemma, the more I came to realize why doing this seemingly simple task was really so difficult. Perhaps Abraham Lincoln had it figured out when he said: "Public sentiment is everything. Without it, nothing can succeed. With it, nothing can fail." I gradually came to learn that it was the American people who began to speak about the desirability and wisdom of having wolves in Yellowstone. Director Mott knew this when he encouraged us to educate our citizens about wolves; he said those citizens would then never fail us. We, and many of our friends like Renee Askins and Hank Fischer, initiated that education, and when enough of the citizens learned, they didn't fail us. We finally came to realize, the problem with the "thank-you list" was that it probably needed a million names.

So, thank you, Americans! You helped us have the belated decency to right a long-standing wrong, and to return to Yellowstone its only known mammalian absentee.

It's also appropriate that this brief history is being pieced together; to capture not only the captivating events that occurred in the first year of wolves in Yellowstone, but also to give the reader a sense of the people who made it all happen. This volume is a great story about wolves, but it's probably an even greater story about people.

John D. Varley
Director of the Yellowstone Center for Resources
February 1996

INTRODUCTION

*T*his book is a compilation of the experiences, writings, and insights of Michael K. Phillips, National Park Service project leader for Yellowstone Gray Wolf Recovery, and Douglas W. Smith, National Park service biologist for Yellowstone Gray Wolf Recovery. Mike and Doug are directly responsible for the day-to-day operations of the program and the care and management of the Yellowstone wolves. This book chronicles the first year of the Yellowstone wolf restoration.

The majority of the photography comes from Teri O'Neill and myself. It has been Teri's and my privilege to help document the release of the wolves into Yellowstone. Our close association with the restoration effort has allowed us to witness, first hand, the inner workings of this historic program. We have come to admire and respect the group of dedicated, hardworking professionals who joined together to achieve a common goal.

Many people were responsible for returning wolves to Yellowstone, but a handful contributed in special ways. We asked these people to contribute to this book by recounting memorable moments, as told in the sidebars to the chapters entitled, "Thoughts From the Field."

All of the proceeds from the sale of this book go to support the Yellowstone wolf restoration, under the auspices of the Call of the Wild Foundation, a non-profit corporation, founded by my wife Teri and myself. Our mission is simple: To ensure the long-term success of the Yellowstone gray wolf restoration program by raising funds, providing information, and generating support for the restoration effort.

If you would like more information about the Call of the Wild Foundation and how you can contribute to or become involved in Yellowstone wolf restoration, contact us at: Call of the Wild Foundation, 25958 Genesee Trail Road, Unit K-502, Golden, Colorado 80401-5742. The telephone number is 303-526-0811, and the FAX number is 303-526-0909.

Barry O'Neill
Executive Director of the Call of the Wild Foundation
March 1996

PHOTOGRAPHY NOTES

When Teri and I first became involved with helping the National Park Service document the reintroduction of wolves into Yellowstone, we were delighted to have the opportunity to be part of this historic event. When we arrived in the park to begin to capture those moments on film, we were immediately informed that the welfare of the wolves would come before all else. This was never more apparent than when we prepared for our first assignment: photographing the release of the wolves from their acclimation pens. I remember thinking, "Piece of cake." All we had to do was sit on the hillside 200 yards away with our long lenses and fire away. In our planning meeting, I described to Mike and Doug the technique that we would use and was told, "Nice idea, but nobody will be allowed in the area. We want the wolves to come out with absolutely no human interference." This necessitated some changes in our plans.

Remote photography seemed the way to go. We would set up a Shutterbeam, an infrared trigger device that would fire the cameras when a wolf walked through an invisible beam. We did not know when or how the wolves would exit the pen: day or night, walking or running, alone or all at once. After many hours of careful analysis, we decided to use a five-camera setup with multiple trigger beams. We would use slide, print, color, and black-and-white films of different speeds, and balanced fill flash to augment the available light or illuminate the night if the wolves chose to exit under cover of darkness. Prepared for anything, we went back to Mike and Doug with our new plan. They approved. We returned to our home in Denver to assemble the arsenal of equipment required to do the job.

Two weeks before the release date, I received a call from Mike. He updated us on the release, and informed me that they had decided to release the wolves at night. He wanted to know if we could get the shot at night. We told him we could. All that would be necessary was a change of films and the addition of some more flash units. "Piece of cake." We could not believe what we heard next. "We really need you to get the shot, but we have decided that flash is too intrusive on the wolves. We do not want to give them any reason to become excited." I will never forget my thoughts at that moment: "Night shot. No flash. No moon. No way." We told Mike and Doug that we had to do some more research.

This event was the opportunity of a lifetime, the world awaited the moment of freedom for the Yellowstone wolves, and we had to figure out how to get the shot. We spent hours analyzing films, telephoning manufactures, reading books, calling friends and photographers only to be told, "They want you to do what?" The only suggestion that seemed to have any possibility was infrared photography. We quickly located TOCAD Corporation, manufacturer of SunPac flash systems and makers of a special flash for infrared photography. We got some high-speed infrared films from Kodak, and set about trying to figure out how to photograph black wolves on a moonless night from a mile away. One golden retriever, one black lab, eight rolls of infrared film, four 100-mile round-trips to Bozeman, Montana, for processing, one Yellowstone ranger (the black lab owner), three tired photographers, and four nights later, we had figured it out.

When we met with Mike and Doug two days before the release, all they asked was, "Will it work?" Within twenty-four hours we had five cameras, three Shutterbeams, three relay remote units, and all our hopes set up outside the Crystal Creek pen.

There are times when no matter how hard you try, how important the task, or how much you want the gods to smile upon your efforts, Murphy's Law rears its ugly head. In the end, the wolves refused to use the gate where we had our equipment set up. We do not know why the wolves ignored an open gate for three days. But we do know that when Doug went to see if the wolves had even approached the gate, there was no sign that they had investigated the opening. However, if anyone would like 180 photographs of a startled biologist, tripping three Shutterbeams and firing five cameras, please let me know. Teri and I have the market cornered.

It would have been easy to recreate the moment of freedom. Many—in fact, most—wolf photographs published in books and magazines are of captive animals that have been released into natural settings. All that would have been required was a quick trip to a game farm (a place where captive animals are rented), $500, and an afternoon of work. Some publishers do not tell their readers that captive animals were used, instead letting the viewer believe that the photographs are of wild wolves. Most people would never know that the photographs were staged shots.

Instead, we chose to provide the reader with true pictures of this historic event. All of the photographs in *The Wolves of Yellowstone* are of the real Yellowstone wolves. We did not stage any events or recreate any situations. The pictures depict the events as they unfolded. Yes, there were times that another few minutes with the wolves could have made a world of difference. But, as I mentioned earlier, Mike and Doug made it clear that the welfare of the wolves came first and foremost. I cannot recall how many times I heard Mike say, "Gotta go, gotta go," as I agonized over why I could not shoot just one more roll.

There are many people that helped Teri and myself with the photography in this book: Jim Peaco, Yellowstone National Park photographer, gave generously of his time to help set up and service the remote camera equipment. Scott Andrews at Nikon Professional Services spent countless hours helping us design our equipment and loaning us his camera equipment that would work during the harsh Yellowstone winters. It was not uncommon to work in temperatures of -20° to -50° Fahrenheit. Steve Yankee of Woods Electronics, maker of the Shutterbeam triggers, loaned us equipment, no questions asked. When we were stumped with technical problems, Dewitt Jones, Franz Lanting, and George Lepp, some of the world's best and most famous nature photographers, generously gave their time and support. Vahe Christianian from Mike's Camera in Boulder, Colorado continued to loan us cameras and specialized equipment, even when it seemed I had more of his stuff in my bag than he had in his store. Dave Erbland at Kodak and Rick Clarkson of Clarkson and Associates generously gave us film, batteries, and advice when budgets were tight and deadlines were approaching. Many other people too numerous to mention helped to make this project a reality. We extend our heartfelt thanks to all.

Old Faithful

Geologic marvels like Old Faithful are common throughout Yellowstone National Park. These features make Yellowstone unique and are the principle reason that the park was established.

Beginnings

The crack of the rifle shattered the stillness of the morning. The bullet traveled 140 yards in a third of a second. The wolf's black-tipped guard hairs parted slightly as the bullet passed. Cells ruptured instantly as the bullet plowed through the muscle of the right shoulder, leaving an entrance hole a quarter-inch in diameter. Underfur plastered by blood matted the hole, obscuring its clean margins.

The smallness of the hole belied the destructive nature of the bullet, which left an increasingly wide path as it destroyed the shoulder blade and three right ribs before exploding the heart. Two left ribs shattered as the bullet continued on its path. The exit hole was much larger than the entrance, and was ragged along its margins. It suggested great destruction. As surely as the wolf had just taken a breath and was alive, he fell to the ground and was dead.

According to court records, the poacher, Chad McKittrick, had been out in the mountains hunting bear with a borrowed 9mm rifle when he got his pickup truck stuck. He walked back to Red Lodge, Montana, and returned the next morning with his buddy, Dusty Steinmasel. They got the truck unstuck and popped a couple early morning beers to celebrate.

As they were driving out of the gully, they spotted the wolf.

McKittrick stopped the truck, retrieved the rifle from the pickup bed, propped it on the open door, sighted in on the wolf with the scope, and fired a single shot. His aim was good.

The poacher and his partner walked up the hill to look at the animal. As the sound of the shot faded away, the reverberations of what they had done began to set in. The poacher had never shot a wolf before, let alone one that was part of the historic effort to restore the species to Yellowstone. His partner said, "Chad, this is a big fucking deal."

The poacher and his partner left the carcass, drove to Red Lodge, stopped at a gas station to get gas and a twelve-pack, then talked over what they should do.

They decided to drive back up into the mountains, park the truck, and walk up the hill to the carcass a second time. They were nervous and made sure that no one was watching before dragging the animal into the bed of the pickup. The poacher started the truck and they drove off.

McKittrick stopped the truck along a creek and used his knife to remove the radio collar from the wolf's neck; later, the poacher would throw the wolf's radio collar in a stream culvert. Then the two men used bailing wire to string up the wolf between two large trees. They wrapped the wire tightly around the animal's immense paws, which were as large as their own hands. Indeed, everything about the wolf was big, and the men had to stand on the tailgate of the truck to lift the carcass high enough to prevent the hind legs from dragging on the ground. They used a skinning knife and made a cut around the wolf's neck. Slowly, they pulled the hide back and off the wolf's body, and used their knife and hands to separate it from the underlying connective tissue. They tossed the hide in the bed of the truck and untied the carcass from the trees. They cut off the head and pitched it in the truck bed alongside the hide. They dragged the carcass to some bushes and left it there.

The war on the wolf was supposed to be over, at least many believed that was what was signaled by the Yellowstone wolf restoration project. The murder of wolf #10 indicated otherwise.

∞

Yellowstone National Park was established in 1872 by an act of Congress. It was a place of tremendous geologic

Above: **Yellowstone ranger with wolf pups, 1922**
Mr. Sam Woodring, the first Chief Ranger of Yellowstone Park, plays with gray wolf pups that had been dug out of their den on a hill along Blacktail Deer Creek in 1922. These pups were brought to park headquarters in Mammoth, Wyoming, for one week. During this time, they were on display and often were the subject of people's affection. They eventually were killed as part of the park's predator control program. (Photo © National Park Service)

Above: **Soldiers with wolf pelt, circa 1920s**
U.S. Army personnel proudly show off the remains of a dead wolf while standing in front of the Soda Butte military station. (Photo © National Park Service)

marvels, stunning scenery, and boundless wildlife. Yet, setting aside 2,200,000 acres of land simply because it was wilderness for the "benefit and enjoyment of the people" was a radical experiment in public stewardship. Yellowstone was established based on a belief that the relationship between people and nature should be characterized by utility. This led many people, however, to exploit nature without restraint; it was as though their relationship with nature was void of ethics.

This ethical void was painfully obvious in Yellowstone. From 1872 until 1886, the experiment in public stewardship fared poorly. Yellowstone was a lawless land where natural resources were raped and pillaged; wolves, coyotes, and mountain lions were especially persecuted. In 1880, Yellowstone Superintendent Philetus Norris wrote in his annual report that "the large ferocious gray or buffalo wolf, and the sneaking, snarling coyote . . . were once exceedingly numerous in all portions of the park but the value of their hides and their easy slaughter with strychnine-poisoned carcasses of animals have nearly led to their extinction." People still believed the wilderness was there for them to exploit. They saw themselves separate from nature, and this justified any human action toward the environment—even wholesale slaughter in a national park.

The United States has always been a country of varied opinions and beliefs, and some citizens of the day were outraged at the widespread killing of wildlife in

THE WHITE HOUSE
WASHINGTON

January 22, 1908.

Dear General Young:

(mountain lions)

I do not think any more cougars should be killed in the park. Game is abundant. We want to profit by what has happened in the English preserves, where it proved to be bad for the grouse itself to kill off all the peregrine falcons and all the other birds of prey. It may be advisable, in case the ranks of the deer and antelope right around the Springs should be too heavily killed out, to kill some of the cougars there, but in the rest of the park I certainly would not kill any mountain lions. On the contrary, they ought to be let alone.

Sincerely yours,

Theodore Roosevelt

President Roosevelt letter

In 1908, President Theodore Roosevelt wrote to Yellowstone Superintendent Lt.-Gen. S. B. M. Young, asking the U.S. Army to stop killing predators in Yellowstone. The letter was ignored.

December 1st 3.

The bearer, Mr. Cruse Black, employed as assistant buffalo keeper in the Park, has permission to shoot, trap or poison mountain lions, wolves, and coyotes in the Park, and to keep an unsealed rifle in his possession for this purpose.

Great care will be used not to shoot so as to injure anything except the animals mentioned.

Lieutenant-Colonel, First Cavalry,
Acting Superintendent.

Turned in May 16th '14
report
70 Coyote.
1 Lion

Wolf hunting permit, 1914

A letter of permission from Yellowstone's Acting Superintendent allowing Emmigrant, Montana, scout Cruse Black to "shoot, trap or poison mountain lions, wolves, and coyotes" in the park.

Yellowstone. The public outcry prompted the government to assign the U.S. Army to patrol the park and to stop the illegal abuses. But the Army lacked legislative authority, so it could do no more than make life difficult for the poachers. Fortunately, the Lacey Act of 1894 prohibited the wanton destruction of animals in the park, giving the Army the authority it needed.

Old ideas die hard, however, and predatory animals were excluded from the Lacey Act's protective cloak. The Army continued to slaughter predators legally; from 1904 to 1908, soldiers killed 63 mountain lions and 196 coyotes. This hunting took place despite a softening in conservationists' sentiment toward predators. In 1908, President Theodore Roosevelt challenged the Army to stop the killing, but his request was ignored. During the next nine years, 23 lions, 1,188 coyotes, and 18 wolves were killed.

In 1916, the National Park Service was formed, and it assumed responsibility for Yellowstone in 1918. But the Park Service retained the Army's opinion toward predators, and it actively continued the control program. In 1922, Superintendent Horace Albright wrote, "It is evident that the work of controlling predators must be vigorously prosecuted by the most effective means available." From 1918 to 1935, government scouts killed 35 lions, 2,968 coyotes, and 114 wolves.

In 1933, the Park Service adopted an enlightened policy that stopped the needless killing, stating in part that "no native predator shall be destroyed on account of its normal utilization of any other park animal." Unfortunately the policy was too little, too late. By the mid-1930s, the last wolf pack had disappeared from the valleys and mountains of Yellowstone.

Today, the Park Service is not proud of the role it played in destroying predators. But predator control was part of a complex evolution within the Park Service, as it wrestled with the management of sites like Yellowstone.

BIRTH OF A NEW PHILOSOPHY

The most significant document concerning the ever-evolving philosophy behind park management is a 1963 report entitled "Wildlife Management in the National Parks," commonly referred to as the Leopold Report after Dr. Starker Leopold, chairman of the Interior Secretary's Advisory Board. The report collected the many random thoughts on management and provided a clear statement of park goals: "As a primary goal, we would recommend that the biotic associations within each park be maintained, or where necessary recreated."

Leopold and his colleagues had a vision. They knew that the goal was not entirely achievable, as some primitive aspects of America were already gone forever. But Leopold and his colleagues remained committed to the idea, and asserted that whenever possible "a reasonable illusion of primitive America" should be maintained.

Through the resilience of nature and despite the early

Wolf hunter's paycheck, 1916

A paycheck from the Interior Department to wolf hunter Donald Stevenson, who was hired by the National Park Service to kill predators in Yellowstone.

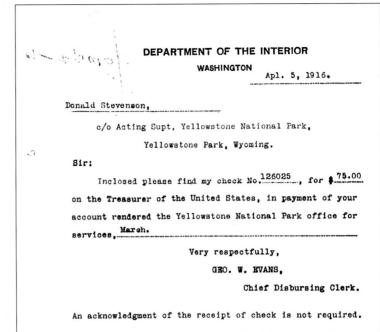

DEPARTMENT OF THE INTERIOR

WASHINGTON

Apl. 5, 1916.

Donald Stevenson,

    c/o Acting Supt, Yellowstone National Park,

    Yellowstone Park, Wyoming.

Sir:

    Inclosed please find my check No.126025, for $75.00 on the Treasurer of the United States, in payment of your account rendered the Yellowstone National Park office for services, March.

        Very respectfully,

        GEO. W. EVANS,

            Chief Disbursing Clerk.

An acknowledgment of the receipt of check is not required.

---

decades of abuse, Yellowstone's ecosystem remained largely complete—with one notable exception, the wolf.

The first official meeting to discuss Yellowstone wolf restoration took place in 1972. Assistant Interior Secretary Nat Reed organized the meeting and involved authorities on conservation and predators. The result was the initiation of a study to determine if there were any wolves still in Yellowstone. Biologist John Weaver concluded the study in 1978, stating that "the wolf niche appears essentially vacant. Therefore, I recommend restoring this native predator by introducing wolves to Yellowstone." By 1980, a plan to recover the gray wolf throughout the Rocky Mountain Region of Montana, Wyoming, and Idaho was approved. This plan was revised in 1987, and specifically called for reintroducing wolves to Yellowstone.

In 1989, Utah Congressman Wayne Owens introduced a bill requiring the Interior Department, of which the National Park Service is a branch, to prepare an Environmental Impact Statement (EIS) on Yellowstone wolf restoration. For years the EIS was talked about but never authorized. In the meantime, Congress did authorize funding two reports aimed at resolving the many questions that surrounded wolf restoration. These reports, entitled "Wolves for Yellowstone?" laid the groundwork for the EIS that was eventually authorized in 1991.

Authorization of the EIS initiated what would become one of the most extensive public processes concerning a natural resource issue ever conducted. The EIS took two and one-half years to complete and covered all aspects related to reintroduction of wolves to Yellowstone and central Idaho. During that time, the EIS team held more than 130 hearings and meetings, and considered 160,000 public comments from all fifty states and forty foreign countries.

The EIS was completed in April 1994. Within two months, Interior Secretary Bruce Babbitt and Agriculture Secretary Michael Espy signed a "Record of Decision and Statement of Findings on the EIS." With a few strokes of the pen, the Yellowstone wolf restoration was officially endorsed.

AN ETHIC OF RESPONSIBILITY

Of course, it had taken far more than two signatures to start the wolf restoration project. Many difficult battles were fought and won before Secretaries Babbitt and Espy could approve the project. Nothing less than a major shift in public attitude had to occur before one could imagine the howl of the wolf echoing once again through the valleys and forests of Yellowstone.

Wolf restoration represents a revolutionary change in how we view ourselves in relation to nature. Before Babbitt and Espy could signal support, our country had to abandon the view that humans have the right to exploit nature without responsibility. Indeed, wolf restoration tacitly acknowledges that we, as human beings, must be responsible for our violation of nature.

Wolf restoration is the embodiment of an ethic of responsibility, and there is no better place to exercise such an ethic than Yellowstone National Park, which inspired our country's clarion call for responsibility for more than 100 years. The wolf's restoration to Yellowstone carries deep symbolism. It reminds me of the words of Dr. E. O. Wilson, one of the world's great biologists: "There can be no purpose more inspiriting than to begin the age of restoration, reweaving the wondrous diversity of life that still surrounds us."

Top: **Mammoth Hot Springs**
Geologic marvels like the pools at Mammoth Hot Springs are ever-changing due to constant geothermal activity. Yellowstone is home to more geothermal features that any other area on earth.

Above: **Sunset in Hayden Valley**
The stunning scenery of Yellowstone attracts millions of visitors every year. Hayden Valley is a magical place, especially during a late-winter sunset when temperatures can drop as low as -30° to -50° Fahrenheit.

17

March 28
Went to vacinity of Wolf den. two Wolves heard Howl did not get a shot. Fished for provisions in P.M.   18 miles

March 29
Hunted more Wolf dens
          14 mile

March 30
Went to vacinity of Wolf den One Large White Wolf seen did not get a shot. 11 mountain Sheep noted in good condition.
          18 miles

March 31
From Hell Roaring Cabin to Black Tail Cabin.
     3 otter seen   11 deu seen
          12 miles

Above: **Wolf hunter's journal, 1916**
A page from the journal of wolf hunter Donald Stevenson. On March 30, he notes, "One Large White Wolf seen did not get a shot."

Right: **Alpha male #10**
Largely through the resilience of nature and despite early decades of abuse, Yellowstone remained true to its original ecosystem with one notable exception—the wolf. Unlike most natural areas, Yellowstone could become more than an illusion if only the wolf could be restored. Alpha male #10 was from the first 1995 group of wolves reintroduced to the park.

YELLOWSTONE WOLF REINTRODUCTION CHRONOLOGY

1872: Yellowstone National Park created by Congress to preserve its "natural curiosities, or wonders" and prohibit "wanton destruction" of its fish and game. Ignoring the intent of Congress, hunters continue killing thousands of elk and other ungulates and poisoning their carcasses to kill wolves, lions, and coyotes for pelts.

1914: Yellowstone wolf extirpation campaign begins after Congress appropriates funds for "destroying wolves, prairie dogs, and other animals injurious to agriculture and animal husbandry" on public lands. This act of Congress signaled the beginning of the war against wolves in the West.

1926: Two wolf pups are trapped on a bison carcass, the last of at least 132 wolves killed during Yellowstone's war against the wolves.

1933: U.S. National Park Service adopts a policy to stop the killing of predators.

1935: Yellowstone Park adheres to National Park Service policy and terminates predator control program.

1944: Noted biologist Aldo Leopold advocates wolf restoration to Yellowstone ecosystem and other large western wilderness areas.

1968: Canadian wolf expert Douglas H. Pimlott in *Defenders* magazine advocates wolf reintroduction to Yellowstone and to Canada's Banff and Jasper National Parks.

1972: President Richard Nixon prohibits the use of poisons on public lands. U.S. Environmental Protection Agency extends the prohibition to private lands.

1973: Congress enacts Endangered Species Act, mandating recovery planning for endangered and threatened species. The Rocky Mountain wolf (*Canis lupus irremotus*), the original wolf of Yellowstone, is listed as endangered.

1975: Federal government establishes Rocky Mountain wolf recovery team. Yellowstone prepares an environmental assessment on wolf recovery.

1978: In a monograph written for the National Park Service, biologist John Weaver concludes that wolves are no longer present in Yellowstone Park and recommends reintroduction. The gray wolf (*Canis lupus*) is listed as endangered throughout the United States, except in northern Minnesota, where it is listed as threatened.

1980: First Rocky Mountain wolf recovery plan is completed by the U.S. Fish and Wildlife Service.

1985: Defenders of Wildlife sponsors Science Museum of Minnesota's "Wolves and Humans" exhibit in Yellowstone National Park and Boise, Idaho. Exhibit is seen by 215,000 park visitors. National Park Service Director William Mott expresses support for reintroducing wolves to Yellowstone. University of Montana survey determines that six of every seven visitors supports restoring wolves to Yellowstone.

1986: Wolf authority L. David Mech, in a *Defenders* magazine interview, advocates Yellowstone reintroduction.

1987: Utah Representative Wayne Owens introduces legislation to initiate wolf restoration to Yellowstone. U.S. Fish and Wildlife Service approves revised Rocky Mountain wolf recovery plan calling for Yellowstone reintroduction. Defenders of Wildlife begins compensating Montana ranchers for verified livestock losses to wolves.

1988: Idaho Senator Jim McClure supports restoration of wolves to Yellowstone if rancher interests are protected. Congress directs National Park Service to study potential impacts of Yellowstone wolf reintroduction.

1989: Congressman Owens introduces legislation requiring government to prepare Environmental Impact Statement (EIS) concerning wolf restoration to Yellowstone.

1990: National Park Service publishes "Wolves for Yellowstone?" studies ordered by Congress. Defenders of Wildlife announces establishment of $100,000 wolf compensation fund. Interior Secretary Manuel Lujan, Jr., appoints Defenders of Wildlife's Hank Fischer to new Wolf Management Committee to develop a plan for restoring wolves to Yellowstone. Senator McClure introduces wolf reintroduction bill.

1991: Defenders of Wildlife sues to force reintroduction of wolves to Yellowstone, but the lawsuit is dismissed. Congress appropriates funds for Yellowstone EIS. Wolf Management Committee submits restoration plan to Congress. Congress ignores plan.

1992: First EIS hearings held with strong presence of wolf supporters. Defenders of Wildlife sets up "Vote Wolf" booth in Yellowstone Park to collect visitors' signatures. Defenders of Wildlife establishes wolf reward program to pay landowners $5,000 for allowing wolves to breed successfully on their property. Congress directs agencies to complete EIS by January 1994.

1993: Draft Yellowstone wolf EIS completed. By the end of the review period, 160,284 comments are received. Defenders of Wildlife delivers to the Interior Secretary 70,000 ballots supporting wolf restoration. U.S. Fish and Wildlife Service proposes starting Yellowstone and Idaho wolf restoration projects in October 1994.

1994: During May, the final Yellowstone wolf EIS is completed. On June 15, Interior Secretary Bruce Babbitt signs EIS Record of Decision and Statement of Findings for the restoration of wolves to Yellowstone and central Idaho. On July 19, Agriculture Secretary Mike Espy also signs Record of Decision. August 16, the proposed rules for restoring wolves to Yellowstone and central Idaho are published in the *Federal Register*. November 22, the final rules for restoring wolves to Yellowstone and central Idaho are published in the *Federal Register*. November 25, the Mountain States Legal Foundation and the American Farm Bureau Federation file suit with the U.S. District Court in Wyoming for a preliminary injunction to stop government agencies from reintroducing wolves. November 29, government attorneys file a stipulation with the U.S. District Court in Wyoming agreeing not to import wolves into the U.S. before January 1, 1995, and to provide the plaintiffs with administrative records related to wolf reintroduction. December 9, the Farm Bureau files its motion for a preliminary injunction. December 21, the U.S. District Court in Cheyenne hears arguments on the motion for preliminary injunction. Throughout December, U.S. Fish and Wildlife representatives work with Alberta residents and Canadian government employees to capture, radio-collar, and release wolves from at least six packs. In Yellowstone, three acclimation pens are completed, and arrangements for wolf transportation are made.

1995: January 3, U.S. District Judge William Downes in Cheyenne denies preliminary injunction sought by Farm Bureau. On January 11, while the U.S. Fish and Wildlife Service is transporting wolves from Canada to Yellowstone and central Idaho, Farm Bureau wins temporary stay from federal appellate court in Denver, Colorado. January 12, eight wolves arrive in Yellowstone. After appellate court lifts stay order, wolves are released into acclimation pens. January 14, four wolves are released in Idaho's Frank Church–River of No Return Wilderness. January 20, six more wolves are placed in acclimation pens in Yellowstone, and eleven more wolves are released in Idaho. March 21, wolves are released in Yellowstone National Park.

Top left: **Autumn Gold**
Aspen leaves glow against the blue sky of Yellowstone.

Left: **Snow-covered buffalo**
During winter, animals like the buffalo congregate in Yellowstone's thermal basins where living is easiest.

Above: **A new dawn in Yellowstone**
After an absence of some six decades, the most important evolutionary engineer—the wolf—was once again returning to Yellowstone. While the wolf's reintroduction would certainly mean predation on elk, deer, bison, and other animals in Yellowstone, it would also help strengthen the stock of animals for the future by forcing them to readapt to wolf predation.

There still remain, even in the United States, some areas of considerable size in which we feel that both the red and gray wolves may be allowed to continue their existence without molestation.

—Stanley Young and E. H. Goldman, *Wolves of North America*, 1944

Where are these areas? Probably every reasonable ecologist will agree that some of them should lie in the larger national parks and wilderness areas; for instance the Yellowstone and its adjacent national forests.

—Aldo Leopold, *Journal of Forestry*, 1944

Black wolf

Running within its pen while trying to elude capture by Mike and Doug, black wolf #3 dove through a snowbank.

A Strategy for Restoring Wolves

Six ranchers were waiting when I arrived. The coffee and cake on the table and the kitchen's warmth belied the nervous atmosphere. For days, these ranchers had sighted what they believed was a pack of wolves, and they were worried about the safety and welfare of their livestock and children. The wolves were not welcome here.

The Yellowstone wolf restoration effort was built on the premise that local folk had a say in management decisions. But for this to occur, someone had to listen. That was my job.

These fellows were upset, and, during the next two and a half hours, they let me know it. As they talked, my memory drifted to conversations I had years before, while restoring red wolves to the southeastern United States. I could have been listening to farmers in Swanquarter, North Carolina, as easily as ranchers in Roberts, Montana. I realized that today I would not convince the ranchers of the merits of wolf restoration anymore than I initially convinced the farmers in Swanquarter. Time and numerous personal contacts with the red wolf crew had mellowed the farmers, and I felt certain it would have the same effect on the ranchers. I was at Roberts to start the clock and to provide the ranchers with their first contact with the "G-men" responsible for their "problem."

Many people who live near wolf restoration sites do not approve of the projects and are frustrated by the widespread national support. Local folk, who have to live with the wolves, believe they should decide whether wolves are restored. When the ranchers reminded me of this, I reminded them that in the United States everyone has a vote; everyone has the right to contribute to decisions on public resource management, such as Yellowstone and wolves. And this right allows the ranchers to participate in decisions on resources throughout the United States. This was of little comfort to them, however. They said they were not so arrogant as to assume they knew what is best for resources and people far away. So they chose not to participate.

I reminded the ranchers that choosing to not participate tacitly assumes that they could have chosen otherwise, regardless of the desires and beliefs of the local folks far away. I pointed out that the right to comment on public issues is central to what it means to be American. The right to choose is the currency of our freedom, and it is this currency that has made the United States one of the wealthiest countries the world has ever known.

It was difficult for them to accept that the national voice had spoken loudly in support of wolf restoration. The National Park Service and the U.S. Fish and Wildlife Service have a responsibility to listen to both national and local voices—and to find a compromise that satisfies the majority of voices. The strategy for restoring wolves to the Yellowstone ecosystem represents such a compromise.

"Fine," the ranchers said, "if city folks want wolves, then you should release the critters in their backyards. We don't want wolves now or ever, and we shouldn't have them in our backyard." They were not pleased when I pointed out that the nation's backyard was Yellowstone National Park.

As my coffee grew cold, I realized the ranchers were frustrated because they had been committed to something they did not believe in and that they felt powerless to change. Ranchers and farmers tend to be an independent lot who are comfortable when their fate rests securely in their own hands.

I needed to help them understand that our restoration plan allows for and promotes local involvement in management of wolves. The fresh pot of coffee suggested that I had plenty of time to do this.

A rancher spoke up: "It's not the wolves that bother us so much, it's the system. That's the real problem, the system."

This statement caused me to scoot to the edge of my seat. This was the opportunity that I was waiting for.

"Let me make sure that I heard you correctly. 'The system is the biggest problem.'"

"Yes," one rancher said, while others nodded.

I thought for a moment before responding.

"First, let me point out that there was a system for making the decision about whether to restore wolves to Yellowstone. That system was about administration, federal documents, town meetings, opinion polls, impact statements, local and national concerns, etc. In June 1994, that system led to the decision to restore wolves to the Yellowstone ecosystem, and then that system disappeared."

The room was quiet. Most of the coffee cups were empty. They were listening carefully, so I continued.

"In its place another system sprang up—one designed to implement the decision—and this new system is the only one that now matters. We can't change history, but we can craft the future. Right, wrong, or indifferent, wolves are here, maybe right outside this window. And that's what matters, and that's what we can do something about. We can ensure that wolves are restored in a manner that is respectful of local folks."

I could see confusion and years of mistrust of the federal government in their faces. I remembered that the struggle would not end today. I continued.

"You're not powerless. Our strategy includes you as part of the system. Accordingly, the system will be what we make it. Good or bad, it's ours to perfect or screw up. If wolf restoration becomes a burden for you folks, then it's our fault, yours and mine. If you're willing to help, we can make decisions that will ensure that the project does not become a burden to you and your neighbors. You may never support wolf restoration, but you can ensure that it is done in a manner that is respectful of the needs and concerns of local citizens."

No one responded, but two poured themselves more coffee. I hoped that with time and work the ranchers would come to see the strength of our plan. But now it just seemed like so many words.

I suggested we get out the maps so they could tell me what they had seen. Slowly, but as surely as the sun rises, I sensed them realizing that they did have a say because someone was here to listen. Using the empty coffee cups, we secured the corners of the map and went to work.

∞

If the struggles in life are what gives life its meaning, then the crafters of the strategy for restoring wolves to Yellowstone have led very meaningful lives. To say that creating an acceptable strategy for wolf restoration was a struggle is a world-class understatement. Twenty-five years, six different presidents, several Interior Secretaries, and untold federal employees came and went as the strategy evolved. You may think that the struggle was due to a complicated strategy. But some things are not as you expect them to be.

Our strategy for restoring wolves to Yellowstone is not complicated, but rather quite simple. It is based on what we know about wolf restoration and on the belief that local citizens must be part of the process. It is unfortunate that there was no previous guide for developing the Yellowstone strategy; the Yellowstone reintroduction was the first of its kind anywhere in the world.

The red wolf restoration effort that I coordinated is the only program that vaguely resembles what we are intending to do in Yellowstone. In 1986, I worked with the U.S. Fish and Wildlife Service to reintroduce the once-common red wolf (*Canis rufus*) to part of its former range, the Alligator River National Wildlife Refuge of northeastern North Carolina, and later into the Great Smoky Mountains National Park of North Carolina and Tennessee. Red wolves were considered extinct in the wild, but from 1987 to 1994, sixty-three red wolves were released on seventy-six occasions. The program was a success, and today, red wolves once again run free through portions of their former range. Yet, while certain common threads exist between red and gray wolves, the overall fabric of the two restoration efforts are different.

Wolf restoration consists of four steps. The first step is translocation. For Yellowstone, wolves are captured in Canada and transported to the park.

The second step is acclimation. We know that wolves released immediately after translocation tend to travel widely in the general direction of home. In contrast, wolves acclimated at release sites for extended periods tend to move more locally. Apparently, acclimation lessens a wolf's homing ability. Since we wanted the wolves to confine themselves to Yellowstone and the surrounding National Forests, we decided to acclimate them in one-acre pens at the release sites for ten weeks before setting them free.

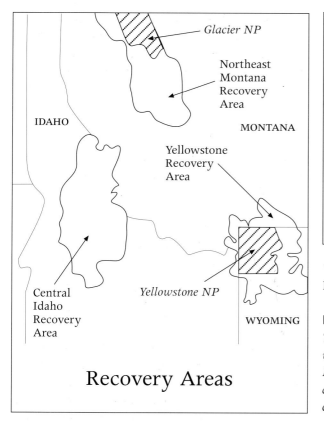

Recovery Areas

Wolves will be wolves. (Cartoon © John Potter, The Billings Gazette*)*

Left: **Rocky Mountain wolf recovery area**
The Yellowstone ecosystem, central Idaho, and north-western Montana were selected as appropriate for Rocky Mountain wolves. When ten packs inhabit each of these areas for three consecutive years, the gray wolf will be considered for removal from the endangered species list.

The third step is release. Releasing a large number of animals over an extended period is the common denominator for all successful restoration programs. Accordingly, in Yellowstone, the intent is to release up to fifteen wolves every year for three to five years.

To minimize the wolves' stress and to further acclimate the animals, we decided to utilize a soft-release technique. This calls for releasing the wolves simply by opening the gates of their pens. Once this is done, the wolves are free to come and go as they please. The alternative to a soft-release is a hard-release, requiring that wolves be transported to release sites and immediately set free directly from shipping containers. The key difference between the two release strategies is the amount of human disturbance at the time of release.

The fourth step is the scientific studies that follow release. Many years must be spent in the field conducting rigorous studies if the affects of the restoration program are to be understood. In chapter 11, I present details of the studies we will pursue.

OPERATION WOLFSTOCK

People often use the words "reintroduction" and "restoration" interchangeably. I don't approve of this because reintroduction implies that creating a population is a simple matter of letting animals go in the recovery area. Restoration, on the other hand, conveys the idea that creating a population is a process involving many steps.

To ensure completion of the countless tasks associated with wolf restoration, staff at Yellowstone Park developed a resource team that was directed by the Incident Command System (ICS). ICS is commonly employed for managing wildfires and other major events. The wolf restoration operation was named Wolfstock.

Operation Wolfstock had four objectives. First, to plan and implement actions to restore a gray wolf population to Yellowstone. Second, to ensure the safety and welfare of personnel and wolves. Third, to focus on acclimation site preparations, information management, and security planning. Fourth, to coordinate operations between sections and cooperating agencies, distribute project information to park employees and the public, and minimize the wolf project's effects on other resources and park operations.

The team working on Wolfstock included staff from the Yellowstone Superintendent's Office and nearly all park divisions, including Resources, Interpretation, Maintenance, Resource Operations and Visitor Protection, Administration, and Public Affairs. There is tremendous support for wolf restoration among the employees of Yellowstone Park, and this was evident in the structure and function of the ICS Wolfstock team.

Properly conducting the translocation, acclimation, releases, and post-release studies will not ensure successful restoration. A variety of social and political aspects must be considered and managed if our efforts are to succeed. Since wolves do not recognize political boundaries, all of us involved in restoration must promote an

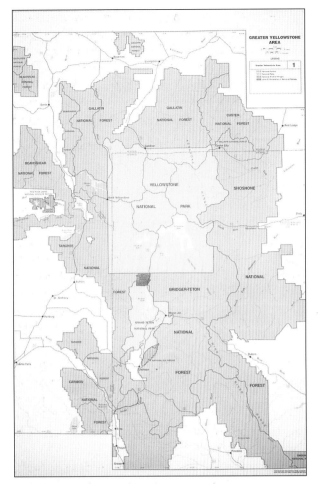

GREATER YELLOWSTONE
AREA

Left: **The Greater Yellowstone Area**
The Yellowstone restoration program is centered around Yellowstone and Grand Teton National Parks, in northwestern Wyoming, southwestern Montana, and eastern Idaho. The area is often described generally as the Greater Yellowstone Area, which includes all or parts of six national forests: Gallatin to the west and north of Yellowstone, Custer to the northeast, Shoshone to the east and southeast, Bridger-Teton to the south, Targhee to the southwest and west, and Beaverhead to the west. (U.S. Forest Service map)

Facing page: **Temporary area closure sign near the Crystal Creek pen**
A contentious aspect of wolf restoration involved land closures. Opponents argued that the project would lead to significant changes in land-use patterns through closures enacted to promote wolf conservation. However, closures will only be enacted to protect wolves while in acclimation pens or when den sites located on public land are being used during early spring. There is no provision in the program for closing private land to promote conservation of wolves.

atmosphere of cooperation between federal and state agencies. I believe the wolf's future and the understanding we gain about restoration will depend on how well the involved agencies work together.

EXPERIMENTAL/ NONESSENTIAL WOLVES

The Yellowstone wolf project is unique for many reasons, including the legislative approach we are using. For legal purposes, the released wolves will not be designated as endangered animals, but rather as experimental/nonessential animals. This designation is a result of 1982 amendments to the Endangered Species Act developed by Congress to promote cooperation among those likely to be affected by restoration. The experimental/nonessential designation allows us to relax Endangered Species Act provisions to develop management protocol that does not disrupt the activities of local citizens and to allow for local involvement in wolf-related problems. As a result, the designation allows us to restore wolves in a manner that is respectful of local people's needs and concerns.

I have been fortunate to be involved with wolf restoration for more than a decade. During this time, I have come to realize that local folks are not so much opposed to wolves, but, instead, are skeptical of the government's claims that wolf restoration will not dictate policy to local communities. Because of the government's inability to keep past promises—and, to a lesser extent, because of the behavior of wolves—local people believe that wolf restoration will negatively affect their lives. For wolf restoration to succeed, we must recognize local folks' concerns, respect their apprehensions, and work hard to uphold the promises that are made. If we are able to do these things, with time, people will come to view wolf restoration differently. We may never completely win everyone over, but we can gain respect and promote tolerance of wolves, which will improve wolf survival.

The experimental/nonessential designation requires that management regulations be defined in the *Federal Register*, which establishes the rules of the game for the Yellowstone wolf restoration project. The proposed rules were published in the *Federal Register* in August 1994. Following sixty days of public review, including six hearings, the final rules were published on November 22, 1994. This final review allowed for input from a variety of groups, including farmer and rancher associations, animal rights groups, environmentalists, and conservationists.

The final rules represent a concerted effort by the

National Park Service and the U.S. Fish and Wildlife Service to respect the needs and concerns of local and national citizens. Here are some key aspects of the rules:

- State and tribal wildlife agencies are encouraged to lead wolf recovery efforts outside national parks and national wildlife refuges.
- After the first releases, the status of the wolf population will be evaluated within three years to determine if additional releases are necessary.
- Wolves will be completely protected in national parks and national wildlife refuges.
- Landowners and livestock producers may harass wolves on private property or in the vicinity of livestock.
- Livestock producers may kill a wolf caught in the act of killing or wounding livestock on private land. The incident must be reported to authorities within twenty-four hours, and there must be evidence that livestock was attacked.
- Once six or more packs are present, livestock producers legally using public rangeland may be permitted to kill a wolf in the act of killing livestock, if authorized agencies have not been able to resolve the conflict. The incident must be reported to authorities within twenty-four hours, and there must be evidence that livestock was attacked.
- States and tribes may move wolves to reduce predation on local deer or elk herds, if the action does not hinder wolf recovery.
- Agencies may remove any wolf that threatens humans, and anyone may kill a wolf in self-defense or in the defense of another person.
- All incidents involving wolves will be investigated. If the rules have been violated, penalties involving large fines and prison time may be levied.
- Land-use restrictions will only be enacted around acclimation pens and, perhaps, within one mile of active den sites on public land during spring. When six or more packs are present, closures around den sites can only be enacted on national parks and national wildlife refuges.

This last point is a most contentious aspect of wolf restoration. Many people oppose wolf restoration because they believe that it will lead to significant changes in land use in the West. Some feel the wolf restoration program is another battle in the "War on the West" they claim is being waged by environmentalists. Opponents predict that the federal government will close public land use to promote wolf conservation. There is, however, nothing in the rules that support such a prediction; the only possible land closures are described above. And it is important to note there is no rule for restricting private land use to promote wolf conservation.

Many wolf restoration opponents also claim that once the effort begins, the government will rescind the experimental/nonessential status in favor of the more restrictive endangered status. The government, however, does not intend to change the designation until the gray wolf population is recovered. At that time, the species will be taken off the endangered species list and managed by state agencies. And then, ranchers from areas like Roberts, Montana, will have even greater influence over wolf management.

In addition to the rules listed above, our strategy includes a fund, established and managed by Defenders of Wildlife, to compensate ranchers for verified livestock losses caused by wolves. Acting on advice from the National Park Service's then-Director, William Mott, Defenders recognized in 1985 that a conservation group could advance wolf recovery by creating a program to compensate ranchers for losses. In 1987, Defenders raised more than $100,000 to finance the compensation program. Between 1987 and 1994, the group paid about $16,000 to twenty ranchers that suffered wolf-induced losses in parts of Montana where wolves recolonized naturally. The compensation program has taught us that if wolf proponents assume economic responsibility for wolf recovery, ranchers are less hostile and more likely to tolerate wolves.

The rules and the compensation fund are a fitting end to years of hard work developing an acceptable strategy for restoring wolves to Yellowstone. The rules are respectful of local folks' concerns, allow for and actually promote extensive state and tribal involvement, and ensure that recovery comes at relatively little cost.

LOOKING TO THE FUTURE

It is easy to lose sight of our ultimate objective: A successful wolf population recovery program in the Rocky

Mountains that allows wolves to be stricken from the endangered species list. The recovery plan will be a success when Yellowstone, central Idaho, and northwestern Montana each have ten breeding pairs of wolves—about 100 wolves each, or 300 total—for three consecutive years. With hard work and a tolerant public, we believe that delisting can occur within seven to ten years.

I strongly believe that wolf restoration is beneficial to residents of the Yellowstone ecosystem, especially those in Montana. Even without a restoration program, wolves are a fact of life for Montanans, as Canadian wolves began recolonizing the state's northwestern corner during the early 1980s. These wolves had pups in the mid-1980s; by 1995, the wolf population included about seventy animals in seven packs. This population, protected by state and federal laws, is growing at an annual rate of about 20 percent. Given the wolf's reproduction rate, wide range, and high survival rates that result from legal protection, wolves probably would have naturally recolonized the Yellowstone ecosystem during the next decade or so.

The inevitability of natural recolonization was a compelling reason to argue against restoration. Natural recolonization would have created four serious problems, however. First, the total cost for recovery as a result of natural recolonization was projected to be $3 million to $8 million more than the cost of restoration. Natural recolonization probably would not have occurred in less than twenty to thirty years, whereas restoration should lead to recovery within ten years.

Second, throughout the recovery period, the naturally recolonizing population would have been designated as endangered, and all the restrictions of the Endangered Species Act would have applied. Thus, local residents, like the Roberts ranchers, would have had little or no opportunity to participate in the recovery; for example, residents would not have been able to harass wolves on private or public land, and they would not have been able to kill wolves that were in the act of killing livestock.

Third, natural recovery would have provided no opportunity to translocate wolves to minimize predation on local ungulate populations. This could have caused economic hardship for outfitters and hunting guides who rely on deer and elk for their livelihoods.

Finally, natural recovery would have been managed solely by federal agencies; state and tribal involvement would have been minimal, further diluting local involvement.

The strategy we use—from the biological to the legislative considerations—is certain to succeed, and may well become a template for wildlife recovery worldwide. Such a template is sorely needed because, as humankind continues its unbridled assault on nature, countless wildlife

species will be squeezed into smaller islands of habitat, pushing more species to the brink of extinction. If these animals are to survive, they may well have to be managed in a manner similar to that employed to restore wolves to Yellowstone.

Considering the Yellowstone wolf project as a template for wildlife conservation reminds me of a Chinese proverb: "Give a man a fish and he eats for a day; teach him to fish and he eats for a lifetime." Perhaps the Yellowstone wolf project can teach us all a new way to "fish," so we can prosper well into the future.

THE DEMOCRATIC WOLF RECOVERY

I believe our strategy for restoring wolves to Yellowstone will be successful if implemented properly. It is critical that we recognize that what constitutes proper implementation changes with time.

During the first few years of the restoration effort, we must spend considerable effort to work one-on-one with local residents. Wolves are a great mystery to many people, and people inherently fear what they do not understand. The restoration effort is most likely to succeed if we help people understand what it means to have a viable wolf population in Yellowstone.

We must be certain that local citizens have a say in how this program is conducted. One effective way to do this is simply to listen to them. We must also emphasize that we will not let the project become a burden to these residents. With time and first-hand knowledge of the federal employees responsible for the project, many of the citizens' concerns will dissipate, and we will be able adopt a less-aggressive public relations program. But to make that transition too soon is, perhaps, the biggest mistake left to make. Without local support, or at least local tolerance, the restoration program will forever remain a struggle.

The wolf restoration project is tremendously important, only if it results in wolves returning to their rightful place in the American wilderness. But I know it can do much more than that. If we are successful, I believe the wolf program will restore a degree of faith in our government. Our country faces monumental problems, and none is more serious than erosion of the belief that our government is run "by the people, for the people." Many citizens have come to believe that our government is run by the few, for the few. I believe the wolf restoration project can remind people that they do have a say, that they are part of a process that is respected around the world: democracy. Democracy destroyed the wolf in the early 1900s, democracy brought the wolf back in the late 1900s, and democracy will decide the wolf's future in the new century.

THOUGHTS FROM THE FIELD: HANK FISCHER

Hank Fischer is the northern Rockies representative for Defenders of Wildlife, the national wildlife conservation that operates a Wolf Compensation Fund that pays ranchers for all verified livestock losses to wolves. He is also the author *Wolf Wars*.

I had no way to know it at the time, but my most important meeting affecting Yellowstone wolf restoration took place in June 1985, when I had my first opportunity to talk with National Park Service Director William Penn Mott.

Mr. Mott's appointment took many conservationists by surprise. We had expected President Reagan to fill the directorship with a hard-boiled anti-environmentalist, in the mold of Interior Secretary James Watt. Instead, he chose Bill Mott, who had been parks chief in California when Reagan was governor. No one knows if Reagan had any inkling how vigorously his appointee would defend national parks and their wildlife.

Reagan and Mott shared much in common. Both were in their mid-seventies, energetic, extremely amiable, and not the least bit detail-oriented. As Yellowstone scientist John Varley once explained, "It was hard not to love the guy. Here he was, a lifelong bureaucrat, a man in his seventies, yet still pure of heart. The spirit's usually been long beaten out of government employees by that time."

The Bill Mott I met in 1985 at a special preview of the "Wolves and Humans" exhibit in Yellowstone had no shortage of spirit. As we walked around the exhibit together, he gestured excitedly and declared the display an excellent vehicle for promoting understanding of the wolf.

My meeting with Mr. Mott following the tour of the exhibit could not have gone better. He was a breath of fresh air. For several years, I had listened to leaders of nearly every federal and state agency provide every conceivable reason why Yellowstone wolf restoration should not proceed. Mott, on the other hand, was unabashedly supportive. Bringing back the wolf was the right thing to do, he told me.

Yellowstone Park Superintendent Bob Barbee also attended the meeting. The ever-pragmatic Barbee tried to bring Mott back to earth by pointing out the formidable opposition wolf recovery faced from the livestock industry.

But Bill Mott never slowed down. Instead, he waved his arms a little more, smiled, and offered some advice. It seemed to come off the top of his head, but it was the most foresighted piece of wolf wisdom anyone ever gave me. Mott said, "The single most important action conservation groups could take to advance Yellowstone wolf recovery would be to develop a fund to compensate ranchers for any livestock losses caused by wolves." Economics makes them hate the wolf, he explained; pay them for their lost livestock, and you'll buy tolerance.

How right he was.

Life has meaning only in the struggle. Triumph or defeat is in the hands of the gods. So let us celebrate the struggle.
—Swahili warrior song

If the wolf is to survive, the wolf haters must be outnumbered. They must be outshouted, out financed, outvoted. Their narrow and biased attitude must be outweighed by an attitude based on an understanding of natural processes. Finally, their hate must be outdone by a love for the whole of nature, for the unspoiled wilderness, and for the wolf as a beautiful, interesting, and integral part of both.
—L. David Mech, *The Wolf*, 1970

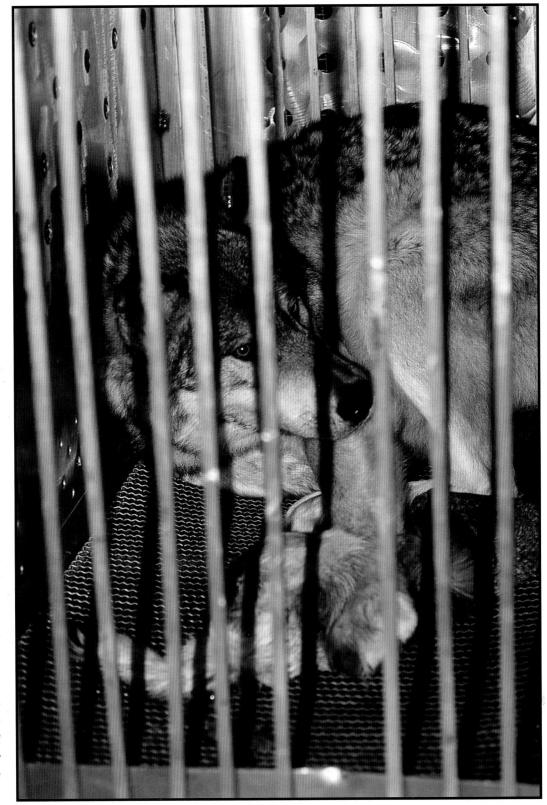

Wolf in shipping container
The wolves were placed in specially designed aluminum shipping containers that were then loaded on a truck for transport to the airport.

Capture and Translocation

*I*t was spring 1980. I graduated from the University of Illinois and moved to Minnesota to study wolves and white-tailed deer in northern Minnesota with Dr. L. David Mech. Mech was a researcher of international repute, and I felt fortunate to have the opportunity to work for him. I grew more excited as I drove to the base in Ely, Minnesota. This job was a dream come true. I remember stopping my car on the bridge above the Kawishiwi River in the heart of the forest, stepping out, and yelling at the top of my lungs: "This is great!" After the echo passed, I heard a beaver slap his tail on the still water.

During spring 1980, the fieldwork's focus was trapping wolves to attach radio collars. The first morning of my new job as a wolf trapper began before the sun rose. A long trapline had to be checked before the day warmed. This ensured that no captured wolf would overheat.

We left the Kawishiwi Field Lab in an old green Jeep that bore an undeniably strange odor that was evident as soon as any door was opened. My new partner informed me that wolves were attracted to "big stinks," and the odor was the collective stink of a variety of lures. A lure attracted a wolf to the spot where the trap was set. All the wolf had to do was step on the trap pan, and the jaws would snap shut quickly and firmly around his foot. Sounded simple enough, but I had my doubts that it would prove simple to get a wolf to step on a circular pan no more than two inches across.

We drove for miles down old logging roads. As we pulled up to an intersection, my partner slowed the Jeep to a stop. He leaned out the window and looked to the ground before turning to me smiling. With quiet excitement, he said, "We caught ourselves a wolf."

He slipped the Jeep in reverse and parked near the intersection. We quietly got out and stood and listened for a moment. Up ahead, maybe 100 yards past where the trap had been buried in the ground, we heard thrashing and saw a large alder bush swaying back and forth. We walked to the site where the trap was set, only to find a large hole in the ground and two distinct lines leading toward the alder. As we stood listening, my partner quietly informed me that each trap was attached to a heavy-duty chain that was eight to ten feet in length; at the end of the chain was a large treble hook that was designed to leave scratch marks when dragged along the ground. The trap, chain, and drag hook had all been carefully concealed in the ground, and the lure placed just behind the trap.

When a wolf investigated the big stink of the lure, one front foot often ended up on the trap pan. Struggling to escape, the wolf often pulled everything down the road for a short distance, before the drag hook became tangled in a bush. All of that happened sometime during the night, before my first day of work.

It was not long before we saw a large, male gray wolf held firmly by his front foot. As we approached, he stopped thrashing about and quietly laid on the ground. He pointed his face away from us and buried it in a pile of leaves. My partner expertly administered immobilizing drugs to the wolf in a syringe on the end of a stick, before we walked back to the truck to retrieve the radio-collar equipment.

Since that day, I have been involved in the capture of hundreds of wolves. I know with careful preparation and proper implementation that a variety of tech-

Kennel compound
The kennels that temporarily held the wolves in Canada until transport time to the United States were made from two-inch chain-link mesh and measured twelve feet long, six feet wide, and six feet high. They were covered with tarps to help calm the wolves. (Photo © Mark Johnson, National Park Service)

niques, including leghold traps, helicopter darting, and snares, can be used to capture wolves without serious injury. But to this day, I am still amazed that you can get a wolf to step on a pan no more than two inches across, causing the trap to fire and the jaws to fasten securely around its foot.

∞

Before wolves could be captured and translocated from Canada to Yellowstone, the Alberta and British Columbia governments had to approve. Fortunately, Canadian and American wildlife agencies have cooperated in past ·transplant programs. Alberta has received elk from Yellowstone and swift foxes from Wyoming to restore Canadian populations. Although the provincial governments were aware of the controversy surrounding the Yellowstone program, they agreed to provide wolves, if humane methods of capture and transport would be utilized, and costs would be covered by the United States.

Wolves translocated in 1995 came from just east of Jasper National Park, Alberta, about 550 miles north of

Yellowstone. Wolves translocated in 1996 came from just east of Williston Lake, British Columbia, about 750 miles north of the park. These areas were selected because their topographic and vegetative characteristics are similar to Yellowstone's: rolling and rugged terrain, dotted with meadows and forests of aspen, fir, spruce, and lodgepole pine. The areas support healthy populations of elk, moose, and deer, as does Yellowstone. Wolves from British Columbia also had access to bison, another member of Yellowstone's wildlife community. Furthermore, the areas in Canada were appropriate because the wolves there do not harbor rabies, brucellosis, or tuberculosis.

A final consideration was based on the provincial government's management of resident wolves. Since the Canadian wolves inhabited areas where sport hunting of wolves was legal, we knew that some of the animals transported to Yellowstone would otherwise have been killed for their hides. Even if that was not the case, because of the high reproductive capability of wolves, we know that the Canadian populations will not be affected for long; the wolves transported to Yellowstone will be replaced by new Canadian pups born in 1996 and 1997.

THOUGHTS FROM THE FIELD: CARTER NIEMEYER

Carter Niemeyer is the wolf specialist for the U.S. Department of Agriculture Animal Damage Control Program. Carter has done much to further wolf conservation in the Rocky Mountains by promoting objective thinking about wolf-livestock interactions. Carter was also a member of the field crew responsible for translocating wolves from Canada to the United States in 1995 and 1996.

The U.S. Fish and Wildlife Service requested that I assist their agency during the wolf reintroduction effort in Alberta, Canada, in November 1994. I was the second field biologist from the United States to arrive on Canadian soil, assigned to the Hinton, Alberta, area. My task was to establish a working relationship with Alberta Fish and Game personnel and to assist cooperating Canadian trappers in capturing, radio-collaring and releasing wolves to rejoin their packs in the first phase of the reintroduction plan. The job sounded simple and straightforward. However . . .

When I arrived, my Canadian trapper contacts proved to be a challenging group of individuals. Some misunderstandings, miscommunications, and good old distrust of government challenged my best public relations efforts. I had to prove myself to gain their trust, and after a draining day and night of posturing, skinning, and spirits, we were off to capture wolves the next morning. We had two wolves the next day.

In my words, my experience in Hinton was to establish a "beachhead." We had to overcome a new environment, new working relationships, media, cold, inclement weather, fuel requirements, holding facilities, and a multitude of situations that taxed everyone involved, sixteen hours a day for the duration of the project. The American team, with the cordial assistance of the countless Canadian residents in the region of Hinton–Rocky Mountain House–Edson, Alberta, pitched in and pulled off a monumental international effort.

My efforts in Canada provided me personal rewards that go deeper than the issue of whether wolves are good or bad; whether wolf recovery is necessary; or which side of the issue you are on. I am a biologist and trapper at heart, and enjoy the challenges of working with people. Conquering the odds in Canada afforded me an opportunity to use my skills and training. I hope that reasonable management of wolves will be forthcoming, so that human interests and resources are not harmed and so positive benefits can be derived from the wolves' return. Wolf recovery requires commitment, compromise, honesty, and fairness.

Philosophically, Stanley P. Young, in his 1970 book, *To the Last of the Loners*, expresses my feelings when he states: "Hated, reviled, and feared, hunted, trapped and poisoned down through the centuries, always with a bounty on its head, to the extent of millions of dollars, as a symbol of the devil, and finally, as the progenitor of the domestic dog—man's best friend—no other carnivore rivals the wolf in the profound effect exerted on human affairs.

"May the wolf never cease to have a place in our North American fauna—a condition that, I am sure, can be made possible in view of the vast domain yet remaining in North and Middle America where it roams at will and where its presence is not in conflict with human welfare. In other regions of scant population it may be tolerated in reasonably controlled numbers. To that end, I have through the years given every support."

*Change is the law of life. Those who look only to the past
or the present are certain to miss the future.*

—John F. Kennedy, speech in Frankfurt, Germany, 1963

**Helicopter with
gunner**
*Helicopter darting
is a tried-and-true
technique for
capturing wolves
that live in open
and semi-forested
habitats. (Photo ©
U.S. Fish and
Wildlife Service)*

Prior to capturing animals for transport, some wolves were captured, radio-collared, and released. The capture crew then studied these animals and their packmates in an attempt to determine the wolves' social relationships, pack sizes, and territory use. This knowledge was important in deciding to which Yellowstone acclimation pens these wolves were sent. We were mindful of the fact that the wrong combination of wolves in one-acre pens could lead to intense social stress and injury to one or more wolves.

As a rule, the first wolves captured and released with radio-collars were not transported to the United States. Instead these wolves were left in place so that Canadian biologists could study the donor populations to determine the translocations' effect.

Pretranslocation captures began in Alberta in mid-November 1994, and in British Columbia in early December 1995. In Alberta, cooperating local trappers used neck snares to capture wolves for radio-collaring and release. Before setting the snares, the trappers equipped each with a "stop" that prevented the snares from killing the wolves. The snares were then suspended over game trails and secured to trees. The game trails were baited with carcasses to entice wolves. Fresh snow concealed any signs of human intervention.

In British Columbia, biologists in helicopters darted wolves for radio-collaring and release. Helicopter dart-ing is a tried-and-true technique for capturing wolves that live in open or semi-forested habitats. The technique requires a maneuverable helicopter and a skilled pilot; the helicopter is flown to within a few feet of the running wolf so the "gunner" has a short, easy shot. Deep snow often hinders a wolf's mobility, simplifying capture.

Some pilots are so skillful, and snow conditions so favorable, that helicopter darting is akin to bayoneting, because the gunner can almost touch the wolf with the end of the dart rifle. Of course, the charge that propels the dart is calibrated, so that regardless of the closeness of the wolf, the dart just penetrates the hip muscle. Because of the efficient and predictable nature of helicopter darting, the U.S. Fish and Wildlife Service used the technique to capture wolves that were translocated to Yellowstone.

Months before the precapture operations began, personnel from the U.S. Fish and Wildlife Service were awash in a sea of details. They managed contracts, cooperative agreements, equipment purchases, travel authorizations, personnel actions, health inspection documents, and more. And as if that was not enough of a work load, the U.S. Fish and Wildlife Service had to assemble a team of top-notch experts to carry out the operation.

Prior to initiating the wolves' capture, the U.S. Fish and Wildlife Service constructed kennels for holding the wolves until transport time. The kennels were made from two-inch chain-link mesh, and measured twelve feet long, six feet wide, and six feet high. Once assembled, the kennels were covered with tarps to screen wolves from stressful visual stimuli. Straw bales and deep, loose hay were placed in the kennels so wolves could keep warm and hide while awaiting transport to Yellowstone. All the kennels were situated in a secure area, where access was limited to authorized personnel. To ensure the safety and health of the wolves, a full veterinary staff, under the direction of Dr. Mark Johnson, was present to monitor the wolves during capture, confinement, and transport.

BRINGING THE WOLVES TO YELLOWSTONE

The first capture and translocation operation began on January 6, 1995. At that time, there were sixteen radio-collared wolves from thirteen packs "on the air." Because of unfavorable snow conditions and the expansive forest, which made it difficult to position the helicopter, the first two days of darting produced few good shots. The situation improved on day three, when wolf #9 and her female pup #7 were captured. Wolf #9 would become the Rose Creek female about which much has been written. The situation continued to improve, and by January 19, the capture crew transported fourteen wolves to Yellowstone.

The second capture and translocation operation began on January 13, 1996. At that time, there were six wolves "on the air" from four packs. As in 1995, unfavorable snow conditions and extensive forests made the first few days difficult. Another factor compounding the situation was the extreme cold. During most of the operation, daytime highs hovered around -30° Fahrenheit. Despite the unfavorable conditions, the capture crew persisted, and by January 27, seventeen wolves were shipped to Yellowstone.

Before each shipment, biologists and veterinarians gathered early in the morning to prepare the wolves for transport. The crew attached radio collars and red ear tags to each wolf, collected blood samples, and administered vaccinations for rabies and other diseases, including a prophylactic dewormer and fluids to prevent dehydration. The wolves were carefully placed into specially designed shipping crates that were then loaded on a truck and driven to the airport.

Within hours after departing Canada, the wolves arrived in either Great Falls or Bozeman, Montana, where they were met by a convoy of Yellowstone rangers who loaded the crate-bound wolves in a horse trailer for the drive to Yellowstone. The horse trailer was driven directly to the trail head that lead to the acclimation pens where Doug, myself, and others loaded the wolves on a mule-drawn sleigh for the last leg of their journey. The exception to this was the wolves we placed in the pen along

Nez Perce Creek in 1996. Because most of the roads in the park are closed during winter, we transported the Nez Perce wolves to the pen in two snow coaches and trailers pulled by snowmobiles.

Capturing and translocating wild wolves was a tremendous challenge, and one that was characterized by unexpected events arising with certain regularity. Nonetheless, the capture and translocation operations went smoothly. The kennels for temporarily holding wolves provided adequate refuge. The experimental shipping crates worked well. And during all shipments, the wolves traveled quietly, unaware of the tremendous excitement and controversy surrounding their trip.

Countless individuals contributed mightily under extreme field conditions, unreasonable deadlines, and horrendously long hours. Dr. Steve Fritts and Joe Fontaine from the U.S. Fish and Wildlife Service did yeoman's work and are due much credit for the successful operations. Ed Bangs with the U.S. Fish and Wildlife Service tended to countless details that arose in Helena, Montana, while the capture operations were underway. Dr. Mark Johnson from Yellowstone did an outstanding job coordinating veterinary support and services. Dr. L. David Mech from the National Biological Service and Carter Niemeyer from Animal Damage Control were instrumental in nearly every aspect of the operation.

We owe the pilots from Bighorn Aviation based in Cranbrook, British Columbia, a debt of gratitude for conducting dangerous low-level flights to capture the wolves. Also, professional wolf trackers from Alaska did a great job locating wolves for capture. Expert aerial darters Ken Taylor and Mark McNay, whose time was generously donated by the Alaska Department of Fish and Game, did an outstanding job darting wolves under difficult conditions.

Laird Robinson from the U.S. Forest Service coordinated aerial transport from Canada to the United States. The provincial governments and biologists from Alberta and British Columbia are due credit for honoring the request for wolves and for helping with many details. Countless volunteers contributed. In 1996, congressional cuts in the U.S. Fish and Wildlife Service's wolf budget made it impossible to cover costs for the capture and translocation operation. The shortfall was recovered through generous support from the Wolf Education and Research Center based in Ketchum, Idaho; Defenders of Wildlife; and countless private citizens who made donations to the Yellowstone Association.

Yellowstone National Park extends a heartfelt thanks to all who helped bring the wolves home.

Wolf in kennel

*Straw bales and deep, loose hay were placed in the kennels so wolves could keep warm
and hidden while awaiting transport. (Photo © Dr. Douglas L. Smith)*

THOUGHTS FROM THE FIELD: PAUL SCHULLERY

Paul Schullery is the Senior Editor in the Yellowstone Center for Resources. Paul is an adjunct professor of history at Montana State University and an affiliate professor of American Studies at the University of Wyoming. Paul is an expert on the history of Yellowstone, and has written seven books about the park. He knows well the trials and tribulations related to wolf restoration in Yellowstone.

From the beginning, my hopes were high, but my expectations were low. In the 1970s, when I was a seasonal ranger-naturalist in Yellowstone, we talked about wolf restoration as something that might happen in some later, more gentle age of the planet, but that surely couldn't happen in the harsh political climate of the twentieth century. In my book *Mountain Time*, I described the prospect of actually seeing a wolf as "the Holy Grail of Yellowstone wildlife sightings." It was something we might dream about, but would be foolish to expect.

I sustained that view through the 1980s and into the early 1990s. As the bureaucratic and legislative machinery ground noisily toward wolf restoration, the sabre-rattling and political posturing kept me pessimistic; I continued to assume that we would only be allowed to play this procedural game to a certain point, and then the hate that had destroyed wolves in the first place would simply assert itself and shut the whole thing down. Even as I took a modest part in the EIS itself, real wolves remained a remote idea, blockaded from Yellowstone by an impenetrable barrier of ignorance and malice. I watched the unprecedented public involvement process, which I regarded as really only an advocate-group involvement process, with a cynicism born in earlier campaigns to do something right; the closer we got, the more shrill and threatening the opposition grew. Progress was matched step by step with heightened resistance to the next step. When we had word that our wolves were actually in the air and headed for American soil, and we stayed up late in hopeful vigil awaiting news of their progress, I braced myself for what was promising to be a deeply cruel disappointment.

With that attitude, I was unable to feel much of anything on "wolf dawn," as I watched the trailer full of wolves pass through the Roosevelt Arch. Intellectually, I knew this all must be extraordinary, but, personally, I simply did not know what to make of it. The presence of the Interior Secretary and the U.S. Fish and Wildlife Service Director did not persuade me, either; these great people were routinely abused and defeated for trying to do good, and I saw no reason why this should turn out differently.

An hour or so later, as the convoy rolled along the deserted road toward Lamar, what I was seeing finally sank in. We rounded a bend and for a moment had a good look at the trailer, a few vehicles ahead of us. Right then, Marsha Karle, who was driving, quietly said, "Precious cargo," and it all became abruptly and overwhelmingly real. I spent the rest of the drive—the rest of the week, as I recall—so jazzed, I still choke up at the thought of it.

Nothing that followed—not the howls on icy nights; not the feeding trips to the pens; not being circled by #10 and then, months later, by one of his pups; not even seeing a free-ranging pack of wolves run a huge herd of elk in broad Yellowstone daylight—hit me as hard as that first moment in the car, when the stubborn skepticism I had nurtured for half my life suddenly evaporated and I gave in to the reality that the wolves were here.

Top: **Rangers unload a wolf kennel**
When the wolves arrived in the United States, they were met by Yellowstone rangers who loaded the crate-bound wolves in a horse trailer for the drive to Yellowstone. (Photo © U.S. Fish and Wildlife Service)

Above: **Arrival of the wolves**
When the first load of wolves arrived in 1995, children were excused from nearby schools to welcome them to Yellowstone National Park. The children, as well as other well-wishers, lined the road near Roosevelt Arch, the original entrance to Yellowstone National Park. (Photo © Jim Peaco, National Park Service)

Ed Bangs is the U.S. Fish and Wildlife Service coordinator for the Rocky Mountain Wolf Recovery Program. Ed is intimately involved with the Yellowstone project, along with the wolf programs in northwestern Montana and central Idaho.

Since it spanned nearly twenty-five years of studies, committees, and politics (i.e., bureaucracy), and involved scores of dedicated people throughout its many phases, it was difficult for me to decide what I could write about wolf restoration in Yellowstone National Park that would be spectacular or unique enough to interest the readers of this book. Moments that remain frozen in mind were when I received word that the Tenth Circuit Court had denied a last-minute appeal by the Farm Bureau to prevent the wolves' release, and, when shortly thereafter, I watched the first wolf run free. At those moments, I knew that the wolves would forever be part of wild country in the northern Rocky Mountains, and a long journey home had ended.

We had already received favorable rulings on other legal appeals to prevent wolf reintroduction, and had begun transporting wolves from Alberta. On January 11, 1995, the first dozen wolves were winging their way south, when the Farm Bureau filed yet another appeal to prevent them from being released or even being removed from their small shipping crates. The Court ordered a forty-eight-hour stay to give it time to review the appeal. These types of temporary "administrative" orders are routine, and many suspected the Farm Bureau had timed its latest appeal simply out of spite. The crates containing the first of the eight wolves in Yellowstone had been carried into the enclosures by Interior Secretary Bruce Babbitt and U.S. Fish and Wildlife Service Director Mollie Beattie. The Secretary made it plain to the press that, "unless these wolves are released soon, these crates could become coffins."

The four wolves bound for central Idaho were also stuck in their crates, and were being held inside an airport hanger in Missoula, Montana. I was spending the night in the hanger with John Weaver, who had offered to help, when the call from the Interior Department solicitor Margot Zallen arrived. "Ed, turn them loose! Turn them loose! The Court denied the appeal!" Sharing that moment with a friend, who had written the famous study, "Wolves for Yellowstone?" in 1978 and had worked toward wolf restoration for the past twenty years was particularly rewarding. It had been more than two years since Congress had directed the Service to prepare the environmental impact statement that had paved the way for reintroduction. After all the years of hard work, of one deadline after another, and of the constant stress of fighting extremist special interest groups, politics, public hysteria, and lawsuits every step of the way, it was overwhelming. A short time later, Mollie Beattie called to let me know that eight wolves had been safely released into their enclosures in Yellowstone and to congratulate us. John and I snuggled back down into our sleeping bags. But the sounds of the wolves chewing on the ice we had put into their crates to provide them water mixed with our anxiety about getting them released quickly despite the storm front that had just hit, made for a restless night.

On January 14, 1995, on the edge of the River of No-Return Wilderness in central Idaho, I helped open the first crate. As I watched the first wild gray wolf lope away, I heard the crowd of reporters and onlookers gasp in awe. They and this place would be forever different, but I suspected, better. I was thankful to be with friends such as Laird Robinson and Leaf Magnuson from the USDA Forest Service who helped with public involvement efforts; Mike Jimenez and John Weaver, wolf biologists from the University of Montana; veterinarian Dr. Dave Hunter from the Idaho Department of Fish and Game; and a host of others who had made contributions, each according to their abilities, on behalf of that moment and what it symbolized. There are few moments in life when you know in the very center of your soul that "This is right." Watching that wolf disappear into the wilderness and knowing others would soon follow was one of those times.

Arrival of the wolves

The first wolf is carried to an acclimation pen. The kennel-bearers are, from left to right, Yellowstone Gray Wolf Restoration Project Leader Mike Phillips, Yellowstone Maintenance Foreman Jim Evanoff, U.S. Fish and Wildlife Service Director Mollie Beattie, Yellowstone Superintendent Mike Finley, and U.S. Interior Secretary Bruce Babbitt. (Photo © Jim Peaco, National Park Service)

Mule-drawn sleigh carrying wolves

The horse trailer carrying the wolves was driven directly to the trail head where the wolves were loaded onto a mule-drawn sleigh. Since vehicles cannot be used off road in the park, we transported the wolves the last leg of the journey using the sleighs. Park wranglers Ben Cunningham and Wally Wines were at the reigns of this sleigh.

Wolf Capture areas

Wolves translocated in 1995 came from an area in Alberta just east of Jasper National Park, about 550 miles north of Yellowstone. Wolves translocated in 1996 came from an area in British Columbia, about 750 miles north of the park.

THOUGHTS FROM THE FIELD: STEVEN FRITTS

Steven Fritts works for the U.S. Fish and Wildlife Service as the chief scientist for the Rocky Mountain Wolf Recovery Program. Steve was responsible for the general design of the Yellowstone and central Idaho restoration programs. Steve also coordinated the capture of wolves in Canada in 1995 and 1996.

My involvement in the restoration of wolves to Yellowstone National Park produced many memorable experiences. Examples include trips to Washington, D.C., to help then-Director John Turner develop a reintroduction plan, working on the congressionally mandated "Wolves for Yellowstone?" studies, attending meetings of the Wolf Management Committee, participating in the open houses and hearings during the EIS process, attempting to plan all the reintroduction details just right, and, of course, all the legal wrangling. The experience of opening the gates of the Crystal and Rose Creek pens in March, together with Mike Phillips, Doug Smith, and Mark Johnson, was definitely a highlight of my life.

The most unforgettable experience of all (or, the most vivid image of all, and the one that is forever burned into my mind), however, occurred 700 miles northwest of Yellowstone Park at about 3 P.M. on January 11, 1995. A group of colleagues and I stood shivering alongside the runway of the Jasper-Hinton Airport in Alberta, Canada, peering to the south at an awkward-looking red-and-white twin-engine Sherpa cargo aircraft. The majestic, snowcapped mountains of Jasper National Park loomed in the background, but my mind was not on scenery that day. For the past seven days, I had been in charge of a dedicated team of biologists, veterinarians, and pilots who had successfully captured and prepared for shipping the first group of wolves to be reintroduced into Yellowstone and central Idaho. Those people stared at the plane, as did I, tired from the frantic pace of the past few days, pondering the significance of what was happening. Riding in the specially designed transport boxes in the cargo area of the plane were twelve wolves that were destined to become a part of history. Eight of them were bound for Yellowstone Park, where they would become the Crystal Bench Pack and the Rose Creek Pack. What could they be thinking?

As my colleagues and I watched, the Sherpa picked up speed, and after taking what seemed like a lifetime to do so, finally became airborne at the extreme far end of the strip. Then it gained altitude, banked to the left, and finally disappeared out of sight as it headed toward Calgary, where the first customs check would occur. *This* was an historic moment, I thought. And after breathing a deep sigh of relief, I took the luxury of reflecting a bit on what had been involved in bringing the reintroduction project to this point.

So many people had labored for so long to bring the program this far. "Such a simple thing," I thought to myself. But, there had not been anything "simple" about it. Why had it been so difficult to send a few wolves across the border and release them into some of the wildest areas in the United States, where wolves so clearly belonged? Fighting a never-ending stream of misconceptions and roadblocks, and knowing that the opponents to reintroduction were fighting against what the wolf symbolized to them—rather than considering the real biological impacts—had been especially frustrating to me, and I was tired and impatient—not just from the past few days but from the past six years. One of the long-term warriors for this cause, Dr. L. David Mech, stood nearby. Dave had been speaking out in favor of wolves in Yellowstone for a quarter of a century!

Our team of biologists realized that the battle of wolf recovery in Yellowstone and the northern Rockies was won that day, when the first group headed southward. I once heard John Varley compare working toward wolf reintroduction to moving a football down the field in very small increments. January 11, 1995, was a date on which we had moved the ball to the one-yard line. The event we had just witnessed was, to me at least, the most satisfying landmark event in the entire wolf restoration process.

Bloodstained wolf #29

The wolves were fed deer, elk, and moose carcasses in their pens. They were fed twice a week at an average rate of twelve pounds of meat per day per wolf.

The Adventure Begins

*T*he night before the wolves were to arrive, we were called for a last-minute meeting. We thought it odd at this late hour, as the wolves were en route and only a few straightforward details of the plan were left to execute. We learned that Judge William Downes at the Tenth Circuit Court in Cheyenne, Wyoming, had granted the American Farm Bureau Federation the request for a temporary stay. This meant that we could not release the wolves from their shipping containers, although the animals had already been confined for nearly forty hours. All were concerned for the wolves' welfare, as placing them into the pens was little different than holding them in the shipping containers—except that they would have had plenty of room in the acre pens. Nonetheless, we had no choice, and we carried eight wolves to two pens, leaving the animals inside the shipping crates.

Later that night, we returned to check on the wolves and give them food, water, and bedding, as international regulations did not permit the wolves to be shipped with hay or straw. Each wolf looked healthy, but each of them was reluctant to move. As we slowly lifted the doors, the wolves did nothing but watch our every motion. Except for their eyes, the wolves did not look alive. Even with slightly open doors, no wolf made a move toward freedom. It was frustrating to not be able to leave the crate doors open.

At midnight, we left the Crystal pen for the second time that day, frustrated by the court action. Returning to the truck at the trailhead, a radio call told us to wait, something was up. Soon we were informed that the "appellant failed to make the required showing," and we could liberate the wolves from the confines of the shipping containers.

So, for a third time, we walked back to the pen. We placed each crate at an angle near the fence so each wolf would notice the chain link and not run headlong into it, and then we opened the door. Like before, no wolf in the Crystal pen made a move. After Crystal, we traveled to the Rose Creek pen and did the same with the two wolves there. Again, no animal moved. As we left, we turned on a hill with a last look into the pen. In a split second, the female pup slipped out of the crate and bounded across the moonlit snow. Something deep within me sighed a gasp of relief.

∞

Alberta wolves are big and black. They are among the largest of the species: adult females average 90 pounds, and adult males, 110 pounds. Our four adult females averaged 100 pounds, and our four adult males averaged 115 pounds, the largest of which was a hulking 122 pounds. Even the pups were large by wolf standards anywhere. Our one female weighed 77 pounds, and our five males averaged 80 pounds.

Dick Dekker, a long-time wolf researcher in Jasper Provincial Park, has noticed Alberta wolves getting blacker. Ten years ago, 50 percent of the wolves in this area were black; now 90 percent are black. No one knows why this color phase has become more prevalent, but it means the wolves shipped to Yellowstone are mostly black, too: eight of fourteen are black. The six other Yellowstone wolves are gray, the most common color of wolves in North America.

The wolves in 1996 came from British Columbia and are grayer and even larger yet. Eleven of the seventeen from B.C. are gray. But, as in Alberta, the wolves are big. The largest wolf in both shipments, a monstrous 130-pound male, came in this second group. His mate was as large as the males from Alberta. She weighed 115 pounds.

Besides being larger and grayer than the Alberta wolves, the B.C. wolves also have distinctively different personalities. A B.C. female that was housed in the Rose Creek pen rushed the helicopter when they tried to dart

Wolf #5 released into the pen
The wolves' kennels were placed in the acclimation pens and the doors opened to free them. Female #5 rushed out of her shipping creek upon arrival in Crystal Creek pen in 1995.

Crystal Creek wolves, 1995
The Crystal Creek wolves of 1995 were typical Alberta wolves—all were large and most were black. The wolves here, from front to back, are male #3, female #5, male #2, male #4, and male #8. (Photo © Jim Peaco, National Park Service)

her, rather than run when the helicopter swooped in close for a shot. This was a unique experience for darter Mark McNay from Alaska, who had never seen a wolf do this in all the years he had darted wolves. Another wolf, our #38, a 115-pound male also in Rose Creek, tore out of his shipping container en route to Yellowstone. Luckily, he was not able to find his way out of the horse trailer. Originally, the drivers of the truck were not wolf advocates, but after watching this big wolf roam the trailer, the drivers' eyes widened with excitement, and they began to think differently.

Since our goal was family groups, the age and sex structure of Yellowstone's founder wolves was a mix of young and old, male and female. Fifteen pups and sixteen adults were translocated in 1995 and 1996. Ages were determined through an examination of tooth wear. This provides only an estimate of actual age, but we know from this that we received pups and adults of varying age. Besides having a mix of ages, starting with a bal-

anced sex ratio was important. In four of the groups (Crystal Creek, Rose Creek, Nez Perce, and Blacktail) we had dominant females, two of which came to Yellowstone in proestrus, which is the early stage of the female's breeding cycle. Getting these older, experienced wolves was important, because the future of Yellowstone's wolves depends on successful reproduction. For the other packs, it is likely we did not get the dominant or alpha female, but we obtained adult wolves that should become breeders and secure the future of Yellowstone's wolves.

The first shipment of wolves arrived January 12, 1995. Six wolves captured in Alberta, formerly of the Petite Lake Pack, were destined for our Crystal Creek acclimation pen. We were confident that we had the alpha male and female, as well as four male pups. Three of the pups were black and virtually indistinguishable from each other; the other pup was gray. Also with this shipment were two more wolves, a mother-daughter pair from the McLeod Lake Pack. We numbered these two wolves #7 and #9,

YELLOWSTONE WOLVES 1995

	ID #	Sex	Coloring	Age	Capture Weight (lb.)
Crystal Creek Pen					
	2	M	Black & silver	Pup	77
	3	M	Black	Pup	80
	4	M	Black	Adult	98
	5	F	Light gray	Adult	98
	6	M	Black	Pup	75
	8	M	Gray	Pup	72
Rose Creek Pen					
	7	F	Reddish gray	Pup	77
	9	F	Black	Adult	98
	10	M	Light gray	Adult	122
Soda Butte Pen					
	11	F	Gray	Adult	92
	12	M	Black	Adult	122
	13	M	Gray & black	Old adult	113
	14	F	Gray	Adult	89
	15	M	Black & silver	Pup	75

The complete roster of wolves translocated from Alberta to Yellowstone National Park in January 1995.

YELLOWSTONE WOLVES 1996

	ID #	Sex	Coloring	Age	Capture Weight (lb.)
Nez Perce Pen					
	26	F	Gray	Pup	72
	27	F	Silver gray	Adult	115
	28	M	Gray	Adult	130
	29	M	Gray	Pup	100
	30	F	Gray	Pup	100
	37	F	Gray	Pup	70
Crystal Creek Pen					
	31	M	Gray	Pup	90
	32	F	Gray	Adult	96
	33	F	Black	Pup	82
	34	M	Gray	Adult	106
Blacktail Pen					
	35	M	Black	Adult	110
	36	F	Black	Adult	103
Rose Creek Pen					
	38	M	Gray	Adult	115
	39	F	Light silver	Adult	93
	40	F	Gray & black	Pup	94
	41	F	Black	Pup	80
	42	F	Black	Pup	92

The complete roster of wolves translocated from British Columbia to Yellowstone National Park in January 1996.

Blacktail wolves, 1996

Male #35 and female #36 came from different packs in British Columbia. Early indications are that the pair bonded, and we are hopeful that they will breed and produce pups in spring 1996.

and placed them in the Rose Creek pen.

The next shipment of wolves arrived on January 20, 1995. In this shipment was a gigantic male, #10 from Rick's Pack, and he was placed with #7 and #9 in the Rose Creek pen. Matchmakers we were not, but this pairing will go down in Yellowstone history, for #9 and #10 immediately took a liking to each other. The five other wolves in this shipment were destined for the Soda Butte pen. They were originally called the Berland Pack, and we suspect that neither of the alphas were captured. One wolf in this group was distinctive. The trappers from Alberta called him a "blue" wolf because the graying of his black fur looked bluish. Some said they had never seen a wolf this color before. To us he was just old #13. He was probably the oldest wolf brought to Yellowstone, and his status in the pack was unknown.

A CRESCENDO OF CONTROVERSY

The climate at the time the first wolves arrived in 1995 was uncertain at best. The controversy surrounding the reintroduction had reached its crescendo.

Three lawsuits were filed trying to stop the restoration, even as wolves were en route to Yellowstone. The Farm Bureau filed for a temporary injunction, seeking to prohibit the release of the wolves from their shipping crates—a legal jab that could have been filed earlier, but now the Bureau intended for the wolves to suffer. The Farm Bureau's lawsuit claimed that we had violated the Endangered Species Act by bringing wolves from Canada. The Bureau's major concerns were first, that section 10(j) of the Endangered Species Act was violated because Canadian wolves are not threatened or endangered. Second, that the reintroduced wolves would not be released outside the current range of wolves. Third, that the reintroduced wolves would not be separated geographically from naturally occurring wolves. Fourth, that wolves never occurred in Yellowstone. Finally, that administrative procedures were violated, and the Environmental Impact Statement was flawed.

Another lawsuit, filed by a couple from Wyoming, claimed that wolves already resided in Yellowstone, so no new wolves should be reintroduced. Finally, several environmental groups joined forces, wanting wolves to be considered endangered in Idaho, and not experimental/non-essential.

We responded by presenting twenty-five years of re-search showing there currently was not a population of wolves in Yellowstone, and that no procedures were violated. Archaeological data and historic documents show definitively that wolves were once present in Yellowstone; it is ridiculous to claim they were not.

Besides the lawsuits, we were overwhelmed with people who wanted to witness the arrival of the wolves. Media crews swarmed park headquarters, seeking interviews and controversy to ignite this volatile issue. Schoolchildren were let out of school to watch, and lined the entrance with other well wishers as the horse trailers with the wolves inside pulled through Roosevelt Arch. People hugged and people cried. It was truly an historic event.

Once through the arch, the convoy of cars and trucks continued on to the Crystal Creek trailhead. At this point, the wolves were loaded onto mule-drawn sleighs and

delivered to the pen. Interior Secretary Bruce Babbitt, U.S. Fish and Wildlife Service Director Mollie Beattie, and Yellowstone Park Superintendent Michael Finley carried the first crate into the acclimation pen, with the help of Maintenance Foreman Jim Evanoff. Wolves were finally in Yellowstone.

ARRIVAL OF THE
SECOND GROUP OF WOLVES

In January 1996, two more shipments of wolves arrived in Yellowstone, this time from British Columbia. In the intervening year, we had moved one pen and built another, so four pens were available for wolves. Unlike 1995, only one complete group of wolves was sent to Yellowstone; three other groups were created by introducing wolves to one another in the pens, much the same way

we introduced #10 to #7 and #9 in the Rose Creek pen in 1995.

Our one complete group, the Halfway Pack, were known to feed on bison, so we placed them in our Nez Perce pen, an area within Yellowstone with abundant bison. One other male wolf in the 1996 shipment was also familiar with bison, so he was placed with a female in the Blacktail pen, another area of bison population.

We did not move the Crystal Creek pen, so it was available for another group in 1996. In this pen, we placed four wolves: an adult female with two of her pups, and an adult male from another pack. We were careful to not place two adult males in the same pen, a mix that could create problems, as male wolves compete for the same adult female. Finishing off 1996, four females from the Besa Pack were put in the Rose Creek pen with a large

Top: **Alpha male #10**

Wolf #10 became the alpha male for the Rose Creek Pack. He was the first wolf to exit an acclimation pen and, thus, was the first wolf to roam free in Yellowstone in some six decades. Sadly, #10 was shot and killed on April 26, 1995. He fathered a litter of eight pups.

Facing page: **Alpha female #9**

Wolf #9 is the alpha female from the Rose Creek Pack of 1995. In April 1995, #9 gave birth to eight pups shortly after her mate, alpha male #10, was shot and killed.

Above: **Snowmobile carrying wolf to the Nez Perce pen**

Doug Smith transports female pup #37 to the Nez Perce pen during a winter afternoon in 1996 to reunite her with her pack. Doug used a snowmobile because most roads in Yellowstone are closed to four-wheeled vehicles during winter.

We were awakened about midnight by the wolves' howling. It was a new howl, one we had never heard before, and very probably the most beautiful animal sound in the world, the "call howl" of wolves.

—Lois Crisler, *Arctic Wild*, 1958

THOUGHTS FROM THE FIELD: BRUCE BABBITT

Bruce Babbitt is the U.S. Secretary of the Interior.

Our ancestors came to the New World prepared only to conquer, and conquer they did. But each succeeding generation became increasingly aware that conquest takes its toll. One of the dearest of those tolls has been the loss of some of the world's most spectacular predators. Places like the greater Yellowstone ecosystem, with its vast tracts of wild land, now provide us with an opportunity to make timely mid-course corrections in our treatment of this land's ecological character.

The Yellowstone wolf recovery program is a milestone project, demonstrating that our society has matured to the point where we recognize that humans share the earth with many other species as deserving of existence as we are. Through projects like this one, we learn not only to appreciate animals we once abused in ignorance, but also to use the planet's natural resources in ways that sustain rather than exhaust them.

The year 1995 began with one of the more memorable events of my lifetime. It took place in the heart of Yellowstone National Park, during the first week of January, a time when a layer of deep, pure snow blanketed the first protected landscape in America. But for all its beauty, for the previous sixty years, this landscape had been an incomplete ecosystem. By the 1930s, government-paid hunters had systematically eradicated the predator at the top of the food chain: the gray wolf.

I was there on that day, knee-deep in the snow, because I had been given the honor of carrying the first wolves back into that landscape. Through the work of conservation laws, I was there to restore the natural cycle, to help make Yellowstone complete once again.

The first wolf was an Alpha female. After I set her down in the transition area, where she would later mate and bear wild pups, I looked through the gate into the green eyes of this magnificent creature, within this spectacular landscape, and I was profoundly moved by the elevating nature of America's conservation laws.

THOUGHTS FROM THE FIELD: MOLLIE BEATTIE

Mollie Beattie is the Director of the U.S. Fish and Wildlife Service. She was instrumental in restoring wolves to Yellowstone.

Most of my work for the wolves was done at a desk overlooking the traffic on 19th Street in Washington, D.C. For weeks I took calls with moment-by-moment news of the capture effort in Alberta: "We've got males, but not enough females. . . . The press has it that one's been killed by the dart. . . . There are problems at the border. . . . We may have to reroute the planes . . . The weather conditions are really bad, so this is taking a long time and we're running over budget, can we keep going?" For each of those calls, there was another from the Department of Justice with reports from a faraway courtroom in Wyoming where a judge was considering an injunction to stop the reintroduction, just as the wolves were airborne for the United States: "Once they're in the U.S., if there's an injunction, we can't release them, we can't feed them in the boxes, and they can't go back to Canada. Do you have a Plan B?"

The wolves and I finally got to Yellowstone in January. What I did there was lift the handle of a metal box that encased the first wolf to be in the park in sixty years. I carried my corner of the box fifty yards up a hill and set it down in a moment of silent grati-

tude to all those who had worked for twenty years to get this far. Then, I put a finger up to one of the ventilation holes in the box and felt the gray fur and a little rib underneath it. Unexplainably, I am prouder of that short carry than many other of my life's achievements, and I was as moved by the feel of the inch circle of fur and flesh as by any deep mystery of the earth seen in its fullness.

When I put down the box, I turned to look out over the Lamar Valley. What I can only call an instinct of the rightness that the wolves were here now swept over me. Back in Washington, that instinct expanded into a new understanding of the rightness of the work of the U.S. Fish and Wildlife Service, and a new self-confidence in my small role in it, understanding and confidence that have since carried me through controversy and contention with unusual calm. The grimy view of 19th Street or the stare of an angry Senator are now somehow less worthy of my comment.

In a right-headed effort to remind wolf proponents that the reintroduction of wolves to the Rockies is only about ecology, about returning a predator to a food chain and nothing more, someone said that we should not expect that the earth will spin better on its axis once the wolves are back, that the cosmos will somehow change. Of course, he was right: it didn't. But I did.

Wolf #32

Adult female #32 was placed in the Crystal Creek pen in 1996 along with two other members of her pack and an unrelated male from another pack. We are hopeful that she and #34 will pair bond and produce pups in spring 1996.

male. These careful pairings were all successful.

One common thread through both years was that no matter where the wolves were, they created a stir. There is something about a wolf that gives it a tremendous presence. Like them or not, everyone is overtaken by wolves' beauty. To most people, they epitomize wildness. Together, these qualities make them larger than life. One only had to spend a few moments around the crowd as we moved the wolves in their shipping containers: "Is that a wolf?" "Where are they?" "Can you see one?" "Oh my God, I see fur sticking out of that one!"

Most people only know the controversy and the mythology surrounding wolves. To actually behold their beautiful wildness, or be near it, is a sensation. Now, despite years of bickering and myths dating back hundreds of years, here they were. But what did they do: nothing. These magnificent, powerful, "evil" beasts laid in their shipping crates. In this day and age of self-celebration, here was an animal supremely adapted to the wilds, but

it was not snarling or banging against the bars; rather, it laid and waited, watching. For doing nothing, these wolves were stars.

I could not help but be overtaken by the enthusiasm. Sometimes when you work with wolves you get lulled into the feeling that they are just wolves. But I, too, was swept up by the excitement, and felt adrenaline pumping through my veins.

One last experience drove the aura of wolves home for me. We asked TW Recreational Services to deliver the Nez Perce wolves to their pen by driving them in their snow coaches, which are like vans set atop tractor treads. Each coach could hold three wolves, with no room for passengers. With night falling, I met the two drivers of the snow coaches to load the wolves and begin the two-hour drive into the park. The drivers had fire in their eyes. This was their Super Bowl. A ride alone with wolves. This trip would be a highlight in their life. In mine, too.

Ben Cunningham and Billy the mule

Because vehicles cannot be used off road in Yellowstone, food was carried by mule-drawn sleighs to the wolves. The wolves had to be fed regardless of the weather. The day this picture was taken the winds were strong and the temperature hovered around -25° Farenheit— wrangler Ben Cunningham remarked that he had never been so cold and Billy the mule probably agreed.

Acclimation

Our largest problem holding wolves in remote pens for ten weeks was feeding them. Off-road vehicles are not permitted in the Yellowstone back country, so we were faced with the chore of delivering a total of several thousand pounds of meat to distantly located wolves. At first the plan was to horse-pack the meat, a much-used technique among outfitters across the West. But an even easier way was to use mule-drawn sleighs.

Yellowstone has a large complement of mules, and they would be ideal for pulling the sleighs. These mules, used as pack animals in the summer, could be trained during the late fall and then used to pull the meat in to the wolves. Hence our wranglers—Wally Wines, Bob Blackwell, and Ben Cunningham—had to teach the mules Bob, Hoodoo, Hammer, Billy, Jeff, and Tack their new winter chore: feeding wolves. Like all mules, the animals approached it with indifferent determination.

Their indifference changed. When we began to drag dead elk and the like toward them, their eyes and noses flared. This, for them, was a new load, and as Bob Blackwell said, "They know that smell—something dead." It took an even-tempered mule handler to convince the animals that this was no big deal and to remind them that they had no other option.

Bob the mule was our blue chipper: steady, calm, reliable, and usually obedient. Hoodoo, on the other hand, had a disobedient look in his eye. He disguised his mischief with an "I didn't know what you wanted" kind of attitude. The other mules had little patience with Hoodoo, so he ended up with Bob, who didn't appreciate the arrangement.

Despite the wranglers working with them all fall, the mules could not have been prepared for their first day on the job, pulling crates loaded with wolves in front of throngs of media. It seemed like a perfect time for a mule to be a mule. We did not think the mules would like the smell of wolf, so Wally and Bob put Vick's Vapo-Rub in the mules' noses. For all our worries, with Wally, Bob, and Ben steady at the helm, no mishaps occurred.

For the mule Bob, however, this was not to be his only wolf experience. At the Crystal Creek pen, we could not get the meat all the way to the pen; the closely spaced trees would not allow the sleigh passage. Bob the mule handler thought to unhitch Bob the mule, tie the pile of carcasses to the mule's harness, and have the mule haul it right to the pen. Bob the handler, cool-headed by nature, seemed unconcerned with mule/wolf introductions at the pen. Following his lead, we were not either. Bob the handler hopped atop Bob the mule and rode off uphill with carcasses in tow.

As with all chores, mules just follow orders. Cresting the hill this time, though, Bob the mule wondered. When he saw the pen swirling with wolves, the mule's eyes and nose flared their largest yet, and, without encouragement from Bob the handler, the operation would have crashed and burned right there. But Bob the handler persevered, guiding Bob the mule firmly to the pen door, thus avoiding the hot electric fence around the pen (and the ditch in front of it) by just a couple mule steps. Bob the mule had forgotten about the carcasses by now, and they danced and churned through the snow as if once again alive. Our goal was to dash to that electric fence and turn it off before we had more trouble. Bob the handler, still atop Bob the mule, still steady at the helm, still cool-headed, managed the mule's prancing and bobbing between wolves, hot fence, and ditch with remarkable ease. We were duly impressed, and Bob the mule performed beautifully the rest of the winter. So did Bob the handler.

∞

There was precious little past experience with capturing wild gray wolves at one location and holding them at another for later release. Most translocation of wild wolves involved relocation without holding on site. The latter kind of reintroduction, called a hard release, has been more commonly employed, and is the technique used for the Idaho wolf reintroduction. Hard release is cheaper and logistically easier. Hard-released wolves typically home—in other words, head back toward their home and travel widely in doing so. Hence, a large area for them to roam is needed, and the central Idaho wilderness is ideal. Another problem with hard release is that social ties between individual pack members can dissolve. In northwestern Montana, for example, two adult wolves that were translocated with two pups left the pups behind after release, and the pups subsequently died. The adult male was likely not related to the pups, but the adult female was their mother, so relation does not nec-

Above: **Elk watching the Blacktail pen**
The elk—and other animals—seemed to know that their world in Yellowstone was all about to change with the release of the wolves. The acclimation pens were built in areas of Yellowstone that support abundant prey populations.

Left: **Lamar Valley in springtime**
The valley of the Lamar River in Yellowstone is used extensively by wolves throughout the seasons.

There is little doubt that the wolf is the most adaptable mammal, other than man, that the world has ever known.
—Russell Rutter and Douglas Pimlott, *The World of the Wolf,* 1968

essarily prevent abandonment after translocation.

Because our goal for Yellowstone was reintroducing family groups, and because Yellowstone is not as large as the central Idaho wilderness, we chose to acclimate our wolves in pens. Acclimation in the pens, combined with a soft release, acts to dampen or eliminate the wolf's desire to home and lessens the likelihood that the group will split. When the wolves are actually let go, the pen doors are left simply open. This is called a soft release. The wolves leave peacefully, on their own terms, rather than abruptly, as they do in a hard release.

The only previous gray wolf restoration effort that resembles Yellowstone's was a project that translocated wolves from Minnesota to Michigan's Upper Peninsula. Like our project, that one used wild wolves, moved them, held them on site, and then released them. Four wolves, captured in Minnesota and released in Michigan during March 1974, were held in a small, twenty-five-by-twenty-five-foot pen at the release location for only one week. After release, one wolf split from the group, and all the wolves traveled widely. Eventually, the wolves settled down, but all were killed by humans. Otherwise, this reintroduction might have worked.

One other soft-release wolf reintroduction used captively reared animals. The red wolf project in North Carolina, and the current Mexican wolf project in New Mexico have released and will release captive stock into wild settings. Thus far, the red wolf program has been successful. The Mexican wolf project, poised to begin soon, should result in free-ranging wolves once again in the southwestern United States.

Our plan involved soft releases of wild wolves from Canada—one release annually for three to five years. Prior to getting any wolves in Yellowstone, the task was to study the red wolf project and other efforts that involved reintroduction and tranlocations of gray wolves. These other projects in Minnesota, Michigan, Montana, Alaska, and Canada helped the U.S. Fish and Wildlife Service and the National Park Service to formulate a plan for Yellowstone. The plan was unique, as it involved capture of wild wolves in Canada, a ten-week acclimation in Yellowstone, and a release back into the wild. This plan depended on building large pens at remote locations, where the wolves would be far enough from humans to feel comfortable, yet close enough to be reached for feeding.

CRAFTING THE ACCLIMATION PENS

The first three pen sites were on the northern range of Yellowstone, the location of the largest elk herd in North America and some of the world's best wolf habitat. No pen was closer than five miles from the other. It was about a mile hike in to all of them, and each site was partially chosen because the pen could be observed from a distance. Locating the pens in this way allowed rangers to keep a constant watch.

The pens were designed specifically for this project. Yellowstone's Wildlife Veterinarian Mark Johnson spearheaded the effort to find a suitable design. Such a pen had to be easy to construct, as it would be assembled in the field, and it also had to be temporary in design. Most importantly, it had to provide for the wolves' well-being and safety. The design called for a pen that had no corners, a ten-foot high fence with a two-foot, forty-five-degree overhang, a four-foot ground apron, and a holding area. The lack of corners was to prohibit wolves from using a corner to climb out; the pen height and overhang was also necessary to keep the wolves from jumping out, and the ground apron was to prevent digging out. A holding area was included in the pen design because it permitted us to isolate one wolf from the others, should the need arise. The final touch was some kennel boxes, should the wolves desire shelter.

After consulting with a fence manufacturer in Nebraska, we decided to build portable pen panels that would be hauled by helicopter to the site. These ten-by-ten-foot panels came prefabricated with the two-foot overhang. All we had to do was clamp them together and brace them to trees or to metal posts. This sounded easy, but it ended up being a lot of hard work. Led by Al Bowers and others from the Yellowstone maintenance division, as well as numerous volunteers during the second year, each pen took eight people ten days to assemble.

In addition to the pens, we had to construct an electric fence around each pen to keep other wildlife—primarily elk and bison—from rubbing against the chain link and possibly pushing it over or damaging it. And in the second year, the fence kept free-ranging wolves from bothering the penned wolves. The locations necessitated solar-powered electric fences, but thanks to the fencing experience of many ranchers in the area, these were easy to assemble.

THE COMING OF THE WOLVES

The wolves' arrival was originally scheduled for November 1994, but various lawsuits delayed their arrival until January 1995. By then it was cold, and the pens were filled with snow. With help from the mules, we hauled the wolves back to what would be their home for the next ten weeks.

These weeks were our period of wolf husbandry. Our goal was to minimize contact, but we still had to feed them twice a week. We fed the wolves an amount similar to what they would consume in the wild, about ten pounds of meat per animal each day. For a pack of five, that amounts to about 350 pounds a week, or 3,500 pounds

Helicopter delivering pen components
All acclimation sites were located in remote areas of Yellowstone. The remoteness necessitated that most pen parts, like these chain-link panels, be delivered by helicopter. (Photo © Jim Peaco, National Park Service)

for the entire acclimation period. Multiply this by seven pens, and that is about twelve tons of meat. And the wolves ate everything. They got water from the snow, something wolves usually do in winter throughout the north.

We did not observe the wolves often, as our goal was to restore wolves to Yellowstone, not study every aspect of the process, especially since there was potential to disturb them. Now and then our security rangers would watch the wolves with binoculars, but they never approached closely. The rangers were there to guard the pens from a distance.

From these rangers, our feeding visits, and some limited observations from a blind, we had a good idea of what was going on while the wolves were in the pens. At first, the wolves tested the chain-link fencing, grabbing and pulling it with their teeth to see if there was a way out. This caused some minor injury to the animals' lips and gums, but after about a week this behavior stopped as they habituated to captivity.

Mostly, they just paced. Not accustomed to captivity and being accustomed to roaming freely, the wolves trotted back and forth along the back wall of the pens; they avoided us and our entry gate on the other side. About one-third of each pen was not used much, and the kennel boxes were not used at all, except by wolf #13. But each back pen area was used extensively—so much that the wolves padded the snow down into a trail and appeared comfortable there; we called it their "comfort zone."

There were signs of wolf comfort in the pens. Asked beforehand if the wolves would howl in the pen, we answered, no, because we believed they would never feel comfortable enough. Within one week of arrival, however, all seven packs started howling. The security rangers heard them often, and evening visits along the roadside could turn into evenings serenaded by wolves. We were surprised and delighted that the wolves behaved so "normally."

It is possible the howling was brought on by coyotes. Coyote researchers noted that coyote packs near the wolf pens howled twice as much as packs elsewhere. Could it be the wolves were responding to the coyotes? The wolves were new kids on the block who were not about to take flack from their smaller cousins, even if they were separated by nine-gauge chain link.

Howling in response to coyotes was not that unusual, but the wolves surprised us when they bred in their pens. Wolves breed in mid-winter, from mid-February through March, which was the middle of our acclimation period. Due to the stress caused by capture, handling, and captivity, most wolf biologists thought that there was minimal chance of the wolves breeding in the pen. We thought that female #9 might, because she was already in proestrus, but probably not any of the others. In each pen, however, we documented breeding behavior. Actual copulation was not observed but behaviors associated with breeding and heightened interest from the alpha male were observed, frequently. Besides #9, the alpha female from Crystal Creek had blood around her vulva, indicating reproductive cycling.

Otherwise, wolf husbandry was relatively routine. For some of Yellowstone's other residents, this routine was about to change with the arrival of this top carnivore—sooner than anyone expected in the case of one red fox, who somehow gained entry into the Soda Butte pen. He probably climbed in, as foxes are known as the "catlike canid." The kennel area of the pen had a chain-link top, and if the fox could climb onto that, then he could walk over and jump into the pen. However he did it, all that remained of him was a skinned-out carcass, the result of the wolves' first successful predation in Yellowstone.

We also observed coyote tracks by the pen, and on a couple of occasions elk and bison bedded down right next to the pen! Security rangers spotted them, and we could see where they had bedded in the snow. Both predator and prey seemed little concerned, as the predators paced normally and the prey rested peaceably chewing their cud. It seemed a nice reintroduction. One of the most exciting relationships in all of nature had been short-circuited nearly sixty years ago. Soon predator and prey would reunite, and their dynamic ecological interaction would be restored. If nothing else, this is what Yellowstone wolf restoration was all about: bringing a key player back and, thereby, restoring an entire ecosystem to its original vitality.

Facing page, top: **Acclimation pen construction**
Each pen was a temporary structure that was assembled in the field from pre-fabricated panels. After a pen was assembled, a four-foot ground apron was necessary to prevent the wolves from digging out. (Photo © Jim Peaco, National Park Service)

Facing page, bottom: **Completed pen**
All pens were built in a circular fashion, so that no right-angle corners were present to assist wolves that tried to escape by jumping and climbing. A completed pen encompassed about an acre. (Photo © Jim Peaco, National Park Service)

Above: **Crystal Creek wolves, 1995**
Not accustomed to captivity and being animals that liked to be on the move, the wolves trotted back and forth along the back wall of the pen, an area that became known as the wolves' "comfort zone." From left, here are the Crystal Creek wolves: male #8, male #4, female #5, and male #3. (Photo © Jim Peaco, National Park Service)

Left: **Wolf #35 chewing on pen fencing**
During the first few days in captivity, wolves—like adult male #35 here in 1996—would chew on the chain-link fence. The chewing probably represented an attempt to escape. Chewing the chain link often caused superficial cuts to a wolf's lips and gums that soon healed.

THOUGHTS FROM THE FIELD: MIKE FINLEY

Mike Finley is the Superintendent of Yellowstone National Park.

I arrived as the superintendent of Yellowstone National Park in November 1994. Most of the work relating to wolf reintroduction had been underway for years. The logistics and final coordination of the imminent arrival of the wolves in either December or January had been accomplished.

I remember being present at meetings and briefings and feeling as though I was an observer. The staffing of the project, from security and feeding to press relations was so competent that I felt that there was little that I could contribute to the operation.

I turned my attention to learning the history of the project and preparing to be a spokesperson for the Park Service and Yellowstone National Park. The arrival of the wolves was a major media event.

The first stage of the media coverage took place at the north entrance to Yellowstone National Park, near the town of Gardiner, Montana. As the wolves were being driven through the historic arch and the flat, early morning light illuminated the hills, the coyotes began barking from the nearby hills. I remember feeling a great rush of excitement and commenting on the apparent recognition by the coyotes of the wolves arrival. The media asked various questions and sought comments from numerous park personnel, including me. I remember commenting on the importance of the event and feeling a sense of exhilaration, but, at the same time, feeling a sense of detachment, as though I was an observer.

Shortly after entering the gate, we drove to the Lamar Valley and transferred the wolves from the horse trailer to the sleigh for the mule-drawn ride to the acclimation pen. Again, the coyotes barked, punctuating that moment in history. Notwithstanding the thrill of the moment, I was still aware of a feeling of detachment—as if I was intellectually committed and physically present, but not yet bonded to the wolves.

The progression of staff and selected media stopped just short of the Crystal Creek pen, and some of us were asked to carry the first wolf , in its cage, into the pen. Accompanied by Mollie Beattie, Director of the U.S. Fish and Wildlife Service, and Bruce Babbitt, Secretary of the Interior, we began to carry the heavy pen through the deep snow. As I felt the weight of the wolf inside and touched the fur that protruded through the ventilation holes of its cage, I began to develop a personal association with the wolves—they were no longer abstract.

This personal association grew strong when, during a rest break, I looked through the ventilation hole and saw two yellow-green eyes looking back at me. The associated smell, feel, and sight of this animal removed any sense detachment from the process. From that moment until today, I feel a strong, personal sense of responsibility for the continued success of the program and, especially, to the well-being of the individual wolves. They are back in Yellowstone where they belong.

Alpha male #10

Wolf #10 was an impressive and assertive animal. These characteristics were never more evident than when, after he was freed, he magically appeared in the middle of a snowstorm. He howled at us for twenty-five minutes and closely followed us as we retreated from the Rose Creek pen.

Release

After two days with an open door, none of the Rose Creek wolves had chosen to leave the pen. Nor had any of the Crystal wolves. Our radio tracking equipment indicated that all the wolves were still in the vicinity of their pen. Mike and I had come to believe that they would not use the door to leave. To help the wolves exit, we cut a hole in the fence for the Crystal wolves, and today we decided to do the same for the Rose Creek wolves.

The Rose Creek pen held the trio of wolves where we played matchmaker: the hulking male #10 was introduced to #9 and her daughter, #7. Our plan for the Rose Creek wolves was to cut a hole in the back of their pen, an area where they spent most of their time and were comfortable. Outside the hole, we'd leave a deer carcass to lure them out.

We set off in a blizzard. It was blowing and snowing so hard it was difficult to look straight into the storm. I brought up the rear, towing a deer carcass. I would take whatever trail I could get. Most of the trip to the pen was uphill, except for the last 100 yards, where we dropped into a small stream gully and then headed up a short distance to the pen.

We had paused momentarily to regroup before cresting the last hill, when suddenly we heard a howl. At first we didn't know from where it was coming, because we assumed all of the wolves were in the pen. But the howl was from behind us, and it was loud, very loud. I turned and there he was, wolf #10, huge and white and fifty yards away, free from the pen. His head high, he howled again, with the snow and wind blowing through his fur. Chills shivered down my spine. It was a magnificent and significant sight. The first wild wolf released into Yellowstone.

Mike Phillips pointed upstream and excitedly said, "Let's go!" He started off, but upstream was uphill, and we needed to go downhill to get out of there. Dumping the deer, I motioned downstream, and Mike, realizing his mistake, took off without further com-

ment. We wanted to give #10 a wide berth, and not push him unnecessarily or move him away from the pen, because #9 was still in it. He was waiting for his mate to come out. Moving through the thick terrain on the bottom of the stream, we realized we were being followed. Wolf #10 was staying with us as we left the scene, howling as he went. Now and then he would break into breathtaking view through trees and storm. For twenty-five minutes, he followed us at a distance as we headed back. This was rare wolf behavior to be sure, but #10 was no ordinary wolf. Finally he left us, not willing to leave his mate, or follow us to more people. I had one last look at him on the white horizon, howling, fading into the storm. The memory of him would not fade, though, not ever, not in our minds, nor in the howls of his progeny someday roaming the Yellowstone landscape.

∞

"After opening the gate, do you think we'll make it over the hill before wolves begin pouring out of the pen?" Mike worriedly asked. It was hard to know. After the wolves had been confined for so long, we could only guess what they would do. When we first placed them in captivity, they tested every possible weak point in the pen and looked everywhere for a way out. Why should we expect their behavior to have changed?

Opening a pen gate and letting wolves go may not seem complicated, but we had to give the release some thought and make it as easy as possible for the wolves. In the spirit of our acclimation, we wanted release to be as "soft" as possible. We wanted to let the wolves come out on their own terms, and get to know Yellowstone in as unharried a manner as we could provide. We talked among ourselves and to other wolf experts: What can we do? What will they do? There were no answers, just informed opinions and a desire to err on the side of making the release gentle for the wolves.

Wolves like the dark. They move at night much of the year. It would be best to introduce this foreign place to them in the dark. We would hike to the pen with just enough daylight to allow us to get up and back, and leave them to the blackness. Our time at the pen would be minimal, and no one would stay to record the event. We felt an obligation to document for history how the wolves would leave, but the wolves were what was most important. There would be no way to put anybody in the area—not a biologist, not a photographer—without being detected by the wolves. If the wolves knew humans were near, it could change everything. They might not come out; they might come out and run. So much subtlety and detail, so little certainty.

Wolves are masters at knowing something's up. They have something like the so-called human sixth sense, only better. We wanted the aura of the release to be as free of humans as possible. We had to try to think like a wolf—no easy task, for we will never know how a wolf thinks, not ever. But we know a little: wolves do not like people, and they like the dark. Besides, why push it? It would be night, so what would we be able to see or photograph anyway?

The Crystal Creek wolves would be first. As a pack, they had been in Yellowstone the longest. Their acclimation began on January 12, 1995, and we would end it on March 21: ten weeks to forget about Canada. Would they stay? Would the pack stick together? It was now up to the wolves, after their historic release.

OPENING THE PENS TO FREEDOM

Our strategy was to feed the wolves one last time. But this time, we would place some food just inside and outside the door, and then depart, leaving the door open. Steve Fritts of the U.S. Fish and Wildlife Service was one of the key players in bringing wolves back to Yellowstone,

so he and Mike had the honor of opening the gate on that historic day of March 21, 1995, at 4:15 P.M. Then we left—and hoped no wolves would charge out behind us.

But what happened next was yet another reminder never to presume to know how a wolf feels or what it will do. No wolves came out of the pen. We went back to our vehicles and checked our telemetry equipment most of the night. Nothing. All still in the pen. The next day, nothing again. The media made hay out of this. During his noontime monologue on March 23, radio personality Paul Harvey called the wolves "welfare wolves" that preferred free food to freedom.

We could not focus on these human perceptions; we had to think about the wolves' perceptions. So, initially, we did nothing as well. The surprise of the public pressured us to want to do something to help the wolves get out. But after some deliberation, we opted for patience. We were on "wolf time" now. We began to realize that the wolves would not use the gate; the gate was the area we used to enter, and they were afraid of us. We concluded that the wolves were probably avoiding the gate area because it was associated with us. Like avoiding a trap set in the ground, they sensed something human about it and thought it bad—stay away.

Or perhaps they did not know what "open" was. An open or closed gate is something you need to have experienced to know what it means. These wolves had not experienced an open or closed anything; they might not have known that within a second or two they could have been headed down the hill outside the pen. Most likely, the reason the wolves didn't leave the pen was a little avoidance, a little confusion. Regardless, we concluded that the gate was probably not something they would use, so we had to create another, more attractive, opening in the fence.

In contrast to the gate area, the wolves had their comfort zone, the area opposite the gate that they used most. We decided to open a hole in the comfort zone, a hole in an area of the pen that we humans had rarely visited. The wolves liked their comfort zone so much, that if you walked into the pen and stood on the path of the comfort zone, you would almost be run over by a wolf as it paced back and forth. Cut a hole here, leave a deer carcass outside the pen tied to a tree, and get out of there. That was our new strategy.

On March 23, it took us eighteen minutes to open a four-by-ten-foot hole on the edge of the comfort zone at Crystal Creek. While we did this, a deer carcass was tied to a tree just outside the pen, and three video cameras that had been hidden in trees, pointed at the gate, and left running the day of the initial release were retrieved. Again we left, hoping no wolves would be on our heels.

...Yeah, RIGHT!

Wolves in sheepish clothing...

(Cartoon © John Potter, The Billings Gazette*)*

The historic moment of release
Steve Fritts of the U.S. Fish and Wildlife Service and Mike Phillips had the honor of opening the gate of the Crystal Creek pen at 4:15 P.M. on March 21, 1995, releasing wolves into Yellowstone after a sixty-year absence. (Photo © Douglas Smith, National Park Service)

Gray wolf in captivity

Even though the gates of the Crystal Creek pen had been opened, none of the wolves exited the pens.

Feeding crew

Believing that none of the Rose Creek wolves had exited, we set off in a blizzard for the pen. It was blowing and snowing so hard that we could not look straight into the storm. We had decided to use a deer carcass to lure the wolves out of the pen. The feeding crew was led by Brian Johnson, in the pickup truck bed.

The next morning at 9:14 A.M., a remote monitoring device placed by the open hole fired. By 2:00 P.M. that day, it had fired nine more times. Apparently, the wolves were out. Our radio tracking gear, however, indicated that if the wolves were out, they were still near the pen. Four more days of radio tracking gave us no evidence that the wolves were actually out of the pen. Why had the monitoring device fired? On March 28, we decided to enlarge the hole and leave another deer farther out, hoping it would draw the wolves from the only place they knew in Yellowstone.

On our trail, 100 yards from the pen, we were astonished to pick up wolf tracks. Around the pen there were also wolf tracks. The deer carcass tied to the tree was completely consumed, the ropes were chewed off, and wolf tracks were everywhere. Many led off into the forest. Dave Mech, world-renowned wolf expert who was with us to help record this unique event, tracked a single wolf about a quarter of a mile west of the pen to a winter-killed elk. On our way out, we tracked some wolves half the distance back to the road. They were out, but they were using the pen as a home base. This was perfect; this was better than we could have imagined! Slowly, and on their terms, the wolves were making the transition from captivity to freedom.

Then, sometime during the night of March 30, or early in the morning of the 31st, five of the six Crystal Creek wolves left the pen area and made their way onto Speci-

Cutting a hole in the Crystal Creek pen

Dr. L. David Mech, research biologist for the National Biological Service, inspects the exit hole that the wolves used and the rope that was used to secure the bait outside the pen. After two days and no free wolves, we decided to cut a hole in an area of the acclimation pen where the wolves spent most of their time. We hoped that a hole in their comfort zone would hasten their departure. Despite their reluctance to exit through the gates, the holes we cut in the comfort zones proved effective. (Photo © Douglas Smith, National Park Service)

men Ridge, about two miles away. The last wolf, yearling male #2, would exit later on the 31st and eventually join his packmates. It had taken ten days; no wolves rushed from the pen as we feared. Instead, they taught us patience, and that, ultimately, Yellowstone wolf restoration is about wolf *perceptions*, not human *preconceptions*.

Why the wolves would not come out the gate fascinated many of us, and for months it was a topic of conversation. Viewing the videotape that filmed for one hour after the gate opened provided important insights. Wolf #5, the alpha female in the Crystal Bench pen, seemed to be the boldest wolf in the group. She often inspected the carcasses we left in the pen minutes after we departed, while the other wolves kept their distance. A few times she was observed initiating feeding. She also expressed the most interest in the gate, often approaching within several yards, pausing, looking curiously after we left. She would usually only approach once, and then rejoin the other wolves on the other side of the pen. On the day we left the gate open, she approached six different times in a twenty-minute period. She knew some-

thing was up. Whether she saw the open gate and recognized what it meant but did not trust the opening, or whether she saw the opening and did not know what it meant will likely never be known. We felt that her reluctance, and essentially the reluctance of the whole pack, to exit via the gate was due to a little of both.

FREEDOM FROM THE PENS

The stories of the other releases were basically variations on the same reluctance to leave the pen through the gate. At Soda Butte, we didn't even bother with the gate. Instead, we immediately cut an exit hole at the edge of the comfort zone. The Rose Creek wolves, however, all exited via the gate. But this was probably due to the uniqueness of wolf #10.

Big, bold #10. If wolves had heroes, #10 would be a super-hero. His nickname was just "The Big Guy" and he was full of himself. We don't know exactly when he left the pen, as we were surprised that stormy day when we encountered him out and howling in the snowstorm; but he managed to find the door, and it was likely he did so fairly soon after we opened it. His mate, female #9, did have trouble with the gate. It took #10 to lure her out, for he did not leave the pen until she joined him on the outside. That stormy day when he howled, he seemed to beckon her. But I have heard wolves howl like that before, and I was probably just reading more into it. Her pup, #7, probably followed the lead of The Big Guy, exiting at about the same time as he, but she, too, waited for #9 on the outside until all three were united before heading north.

By the time we were ready to free the Soda Butte wolves, we had decided that the gate was probably not a good exit hole. On March 27, a crew headed to the Soda Butte pen at 4:00 P.M. to cut an exit hole in the fence on the edge of the wolves' comfort zone. We tied a deer to a tree about six feet outside the pen. All of this took sixteen minutes. We were concerned about how much time we spent by the hole, because part of the wolves' avoidance to leave could be due to human scent and activity. Unlike the other two pens, this pen had a hidden observation area about a mile away where we could observe the wolves' reactions to the hole.

For about two and a half hours, the wolves avoided the hole. They approached numerous times, but they always kept their distance, never coming closer than ten feet to fifteen feet. As they walked the perimeter of the pen, the wolves' course would change near the hole, arcing their route to avoid the area. A few times a wolf approached the hole to about thirty feet, stared at it, and retreated. At 7:00 P.M., when the light was failing, the wolves made a move on the deer carcass. Slowly and cautiously, three wolves approached the meat. Then, two wolves left the pen and began to feed on the deer outside the fence! Shortly thereafter it was too dark to see, so we had to leave. But we were amazed: the wolves left the pen—and went back in!

Two days later, early on March 29, the wolves left the pen for good. We arrived at 8:30 A.M. one morning to check the wolves, and filmmaker Bob Landis told us he had just filmed a wolf running across Soda Butte Creek. Immediately, we wanted to track the wolves at the pen to learn what had happened. We were able to track these wolves extensively and we were pleased with what we found. In the spirit of a soft release, the wolves left slowly and explored the area around their pen. One wolf walked up to a winter-killed elk, but did not feed on it. Gradually, the wolves headed east as a group, and within a half-mile, killed a nine-month-old, half-grown calf elk. This was a great way to begin their time as wild wolves.

Nothing happened as we thought it would during the release operation. Wolves did not rush from the pen as soon as we cleared the area, and they were reluctant to walk through the gate. The pen was the only area the wolves had known in Yellowstone. To them, it might have seemed that everywhere outside the pen was crawling with people. Leaving the only place they knew was not easy, even if the pen was cramped. But in the end, the lessons were ours to learn; we had our notions of how the release would go, but the wolves showed us how it would be.

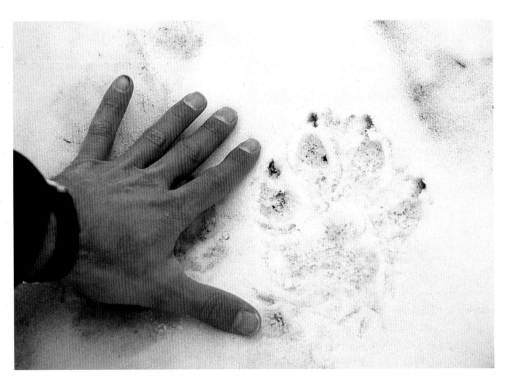

Wolf track
We were able to track the Soda Butte wolves extensively and were pleased with what we documented. Gradually, the wolves traveled east as a group and, within a half-mile, killed an elk calf.

THOUGHTS FROM THE FIELD: MARK R. JOHNSON

Mark R. Johnson has worked for the National Park Service as a wildlife veterinarian for many years. He was responsible for many of the aspects of the Yellowstone restoration design and coordinated veterinary support for the translocation of wolves from Canada in 1995 and 1996.

For the wolves, reintroduction was like surgery, producing temporary discomfort and pain for long-term healing. I would expect, that given the choice, the translocated wolves would have preferred natural re-colonization over translocation. It seems intuitive that wolves would choose traveling through forests and fields over being helicopter-darted, transported in crates, and confined for many weeks. But we all recognized that in the long run, the *manual* approach was far better for wolves than a hands-off approach. Our surgical role promoted healing for wolf populations long persecuted; healing for Yellowstone and Idaho ecosystems that have been without wolves for so long; and healing of a distracted culture by building awareness and recognition for wolves and wild places.

In Canada, each captured wolf was handled quickly, efficiently, and respectfully. Biologists and veterinarians monitored temperature, pulse, and respiration closely; collected blood and other samples to assess the wolf's health; and gave them medications and vaccines to protect the wolves from disease and prevent them from transporting diseases with them. Finally, each wolf was radio-collared and ear-tagged, then placed in a secure holding kennel darkened with covers and deep with straw around a straw-bale den. With all of this processing, the wolves must have felt like the Tin Man getting tuned-up for the *Wizard of Oz*. Yet equipment and techniques were chosen carefully, and personnel handled each wolf in a caring and conscientious manner.

Here in the Lamar Valley, I now watch as brothers of the Crystal Pack, founders of an ecosystem, run with excitement among herds of bison and elk. Their initial experiences are now insignificant, long since healed.

THOUGHTS FROM THE FIELD: L. DAVID MECH

L. David Mech is a research biologist for the National Biological Service. Dave has researched wolves and worked on behalf of wolf conservation longer and more effectively than anyone in the world. Dave was a member of the field crew responsible for the translocation of wolves from Canada to the United States in 1995 and 1996 and is a consultant to the Yellowstone wolf project.

As the bulky, wolf-laden aircraft rumbled down the isolated Alberta runway on January 11, 1995, and lifted off, I heaved a huge sigh of relief. And of elation and joy. The man-made, high-tech, mass-wolf dispersal to Yellowstone I had dreamed of for so many years had begun.

In my mind, this was the critical point in restoring wolves throughout the western United States. The rest would be automatic. The wolves would soon be released and possibly be given a boost here and there by humans. Some would eventually be killed. But, barring a crash in the next few hours, enough of the plane's dozen dispersers destined for Yellowstone and central Idaho would surely survive to recolonize the West.

Natural recolonization is a simple process in which wolves excel. From any given reservoir population, wolves disperse for hundreds of miles, meet mates doing the same thing, breed, and occupy the new area. Around Yellowstone, however, humans had thwarted that process for decades by eliminating any nearby reservoirs and modifying the surroundings so much that wolves could not reach the park.

Now I was pleased to be one of the humans correcting the situation with this planeload of dispersers. Herculean legal, political, and logistical efforts had led up to this flight. And additional flights, considerable folderol, legal hurdles, and much monitoring would follow.

Nevertheless, I was entirely confident that once these first wolves were freed, the basic deed would be done. Like their naturally dispersing relatives around the world, the transplants would be fruitful and multiply and fill the void that had been so unnatural for so long.

My companions and I stood misty-eyed as we watched the plane disappear southward on its historic mission. Wolves had returned to the West.

Above: **Sendoff for the wolves**

A group of wolf supporters gave the wolves a prayerful sendoff. Native Americans Scott Frazier (in the Navajo rug coat) and John Potter (holding the drum) spoke and sang for the wolves. "We want to pray for the freedom throughout the world," said Frazier, "freedom in humanity, freedom in wildlife. . . . It's not that we are siding with anybody. We are siding with everybody."

Right: **Alpha male #35**

The second batch of wolves was released into Yellowstone in April 1996, including #35, the alpha male from the Blacktail pen.

We must learn to think not only logically but biologically.
—Edward Abbey, *One Life at a Time, Please,* 1988

**Lower Falls
in winter**
*Yellowstone
reverberated once
again with the
howl of the wolf,
following the
release of the first
batch of wolves in
March 1995.*

Freedom

I had anxiously anticipated the release of the wolves. Our goal was free-ranging wolves, and most of my experience was with wild wolves; I wanted to move from wolf husbandry to field research. Also, we all wondered what was going to happen. What were the wolves going to do? Where would they go? Would they roam widely or restrict their movements? And, most of all, I wanted to see wolves roaming free in Yellowstone. Few sights in nature are as awe-inspiring as spotting a pack of wolves making their way across a snowy landscape.

Seeing these wolves free would be even more special because we knew them. When studying wolves in the wild, one rarely sees them; whatever is known comes indirectly via radio tracking. Occasionally wolves are handled, but usually this is only for a brief period once or twice in their lives, not enough to get to know individual wolves. During acclimation, we had the opportunity to learn the wolves' markings and, to some extent, their personalities.

Soda Butte Pack included three black male and two gray female wolves. That was handy. The young male #15 got picked on the most. Wolf #14, the eventual mother of Soda Butte's one pup, liked to jump up on the kennel boxes for a better look at us when we came to feed. She was the only wolf that did this. And then there was old #13, as distinctive a wolf as #10, but for different reasons. Besides his bluish color, #13 was also the only wolf that actually used the kennel boxes. Whenever we came to feed, he was nowhere to be seen because he would run into the kennel box near the gate of the pen. He used the same one every time, and would remain in it even if we lifted the top to take a look inside.

Once #13 was not inside the box when we entered the pen to feed. One of our volunteers, Lessie Redman, was dragging an elk hindquarter into the pen when #13 started running right at her. Redman knew that wolves are frightened of people and would never do anything, but here was this wolf charging headlong toward her. She stood dismayed and awed as the big wolf grazed her and ran past her into "his" kennel box. It was quite an experience.

Several of us wondered about #13. Would he stay with the pack after being released? He was the oldest wolf brought to Yellowstone and seemed subordinate. Indeed, when the day came for the wolves to leave the pen, #13 exited alone. Filmmaker Robert Landis filmed him running solo across the open plain of Soda Butte Creek. We tracked #13 later that day, separate from the other wolves. Maybe old #13 had enough abuse in the pen.

The next day, March 30, was the first radio-tracking flight of Yellowstone's new wolf era. Aerial radio tracking would be our primary tool to learn about the wolves. In the tracking plane, we headed toward Soda Butte Creek, figuring we'd pick up a signal there and then move in on it for a specific location. Sure enough, as we flew toward the creek, we picked up a faint signal from one of the Soda Butte wolves, only it was not coming from up the creek, but rather from the area of the Lamar River above the confluence with Soda Butte Creek. Then, almost by surprise, there they were—all five Soda Butte wolves strung out together on a ridge above the Lamar River. They had found each other!

We made a pass, not too low because I was worried about bothering the pack, but I was curious how old #13 was doing. As we got closer, I could make out his distinctive blue coat color. The old boy was number two in line, behind one of the gray females. It was right then I felt some adrenaline enter my veins, and I forgot about all the time in between moments like this. Wolf #13 no longer looked old. There were no signs of his former cowering in the kennel box; he was big

Everyone expected the wolves to "run for the border." Quite to the contrary, however, they exhibited restricted movements after release. (Cartoon © John Potter, The Billings Gazette*)*

and bold and free, running up front with his pack in new territory. Wolves were once again wild and free in Yellowstone.

∞

It was of the utmost importance to keep track of the wolves after they left the pen. This simple job would be the backbone of our entire program: Where were the wolves? When we knew where they were, we could do other things, too, but this was our starting point. There was a certain amount of pressure associated with this task, as many opponents of wolf restoration in Yellowstone were anxious to see things go wrong. If the wolves had immediately headed back to Canada or out to the ranches to kill livestock, it would have been seen as strong evidence that wolf reintroduction would not work.

Because of the elusive nature of wolves and their great ability to travel, the use of aircraft is about the only way to follow them. There was no other way we could keep up with them in the remote, snow-laden areas they would travel. Wolves will almost never allow a close approach on the ground, and if they do become aware of humans, something we considered an unacceptable disturbance, they will leave. Also, even when ground locations can be obtained, they rarely include visual observations. From the air, visual observations are common, lending greater accuracy when plotting movements, allowing total counts, and, perhaps, most importantly giving us the ability to watch the wolves without disturbing them.

Aerial and ground radio tracking would be our main tool, the tried-and-true methodology of wildlife studies since the 1960s. Each wolf brought from Canada was fitted with a radio collar, allowing us to home in on a radio signal. Each collar had a unique frequency. When we wanted to track a particular wolf, we tuned into that wolf's frequency, kind of like tuning your radio dial to various stations. From the air we could hear a signal routinely from about ten miles to as much as thirty miles, and from the ground, anywhere from one to three miles.

THE WOLVES EXPLORE YELLOWSTONE

Initially, it appeared we would need none of this fancy technology: the wolves stayed put. For three weeks, the Soda Butte and Crystal Creek Packs hung out in limited areas near their pens. The Rose Creek Pack did so, too, but not for as long. During this time, average distance traveled each day was low for wolves, about three miles to five miles, and the amount of area used was also below average, at about 80 to 100 square miles.

Then an abrupt increase in movements signaled the beginning of what we later called the wolves' exploratory period. Within a couple days of each other in late April, the Crystal Creek and Soda Butte wolves started travel-

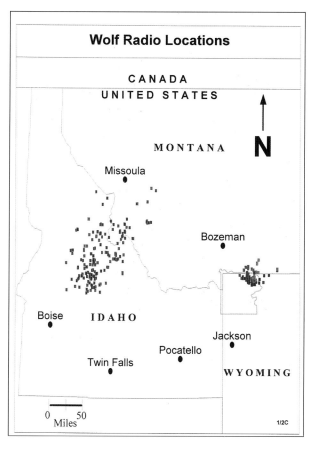

Wolf Radio Locations

CANADA
UNITED STATES

N

MONTANA

Missoula

Bozeman

Boise   IDAHO

Jackson

Pocatello

Twin Falls   WYOMING

0   50
Miles

1/2C

Movements of wolves released in Yellowstone and central Idaho

Movements differed between wolves released in Yellowstone and central Idaho. For example, by late June 1995, the wolves in Idaho had moved an average of fifty miles north. In contrast, the three Yellowstone packs, depicted with different colors, have not shown any inclination to move north. Although not a definitive experiment, results suggest that acclimation does attenuate a wolf's homing tendency.

ing northeast and north, respectively, about twenty-five miles each day. For the Crystal wolves, this meant a foray northeast from Yellowstone into Custer National Forest near Red Lodge, Montana, and for the Soda Butte wolves, a trip deep into the Absaroka-Beartooth Wilderness. As fast as they left, the Crystal Creek wolves returned, but not so with the Soda Butte wolves. Something stopped them in the Absaroka-Beartooth Wilderness, and it was not until later that we discovered that a pup had been born. After these exploratory moves, both packs settled into an area of about 250 square miles, with daily straight-line movements of about three miles to five miles, again.

The Rose Creek wolves behaved similarly, but the periods, group composition, and end result were different from the other two packs. After #9 joined her mate and daughter outside the pen, the trio moved north about fifteen miles, eventually hunkering down for four days in the Buffalo Creek drainage. We observed a cow and calf moose in the same area, which perhaps interested the wolves enough to cause them to linger, but we have no evidence that they killed anything. They then abruptly moved southeast, but #7 did not accompany #9 and #10, breaking away probably under her own volition.

Wolf #7 remained alone, traveling the north central part of the park, possibly looking for a lone male wolf. Finally, in late January 1996, male wolf #2 from the Crystal Creek Pack dispersed and paired with #7. It was

Yellowstone's first naturally forming wolf pack in sixty years.

Wolves #9 and #10 kept moving. After traveling southeast, they headed back northwest and then (we presume) north again. However, after a location on April 13 near Slough Creek, we lost track of these wolves for eleven days. On April 24, both #9 and #10 were seen just outside Red Lodge. On April 26, #10's collar was in "mortality mode," a situation where a radio collar sensor activates a quickening of the pulse rate on the collar signal. This indicates that the wolf has not moved for four hours, a good sign that the animal is dead. U.S. Fish and Wildlife Service special agents later found the carcass of #10—illegally shot, skinned, and beheaded by Chad McKittrick of Red Lodge. McKittrick was sentenced in 1996 to six months in jail, a $10,000 fine, and one year of supervisory release.

TESTING THEIR NEW-FOUND FREEDOM

The movements of the Yellowstone wolves post-release is especially interesting because only one other wolf restoration project used a similar strategy. In 1974, four wolves were captured in northern Minnesota and flown to Michigan's Upper Peninsula in an attempt to re-establish a wolf population there and test a wolf reintroduction technique. These wolves were held on site for a week in a small pen before being released into the wild.

What those wolves did was amazingly similar to what the Yellowstone wolves did.

The authors of the study categorized the Michigan wolves' post-release behavior into four phases: post-release, directional movements, exploratory, and settled. We could categorize Yellowstone wolf movements similarly. Our post-release phase, like Michigan's, consisted of the wolves remaining in the general area of the pen site. Unlike the Michigan wolves, the Yellowstone wolves' north and northeast trip could not be categorized as directional movement. In both cases, the wolves came back, for Crystal immediately, and for Soda Butte in mid-summer. We would categorize their movements after the post-release phase as exploratory, as they traveled widely. Finally, when the Michigan wolves were killed, they began a sedentary phase that our wolves have exhibited

since returning from their explorations.

Another aspect of Yellowstone wolf movements was how little the wolves moved from their acclimation sites. By late June 1995, the hard-released wolves in Idaho had moved an average of fifty miles north of their release sites. Yellowstone wolves released at the same time had moved, on average, nowhere. Although not a definitive experiment, acclimation did appear to have the desired effect on wolf movements.

Besides movements, another post-release behavior of interest was pack cohesiveness. Rarely are all the wolves in a pack collared. Instead, just one or two are. So having them all collared allowed us to examine how often the wolves traveled as a pack or in smaller units.

Initially, one of the Crystal Creek wolves was never located with the pack. Wolf #2 did not exit the pen with

Wolf #13 "Old Blue"
Male #13 was a black wolf, but his coat had turned mostly gray with age, giving it what some considered a "blue" tinge. Some trappers in Alberta said they had never seen a wolf that color. He was also the only wolf that used the kennel boxes.

Radio-tracking wolves by airplane
Due to the rugged and expansive terrain of Yellowstone and the mobility of wolves, aerial radio-tracking is our main field technique. This has been the tried-and-true methodology of wolf research since the 1960s.

the other five Crystal wolves, and traveled alone during April. On one occasion, #2 joined the rest of his packmates to share a kill. We thought that after this he would remain with his pack, but by the time of the next location, #2 was on his own again. Finally, in early May, #2 hooked up with his packmates and more or less spent the summer with them. The Crystal pack was more or less together throughout this time. The alpha pair, #4 and #5, were always located together, but any one or two of the yearlings was often off on their own. None of the yearling pairings lasted for more than a few days, and never did they stray too far from the alphas. In August, the Crystal wolves began traveling as a pack, rarely being apart, through fall and early winter.

The Soda Butte wolves behaved similarly to the Crystal wolves, but instead of moving loosely as a group, they had a "base camp." The Soda Buttes were always located together until late in April, when #14 gave birth to at least one pup. The presence of this pup anchored the wolves to a den, and other than the pup's mother, #14, the other wolves came and went from this centralized location singly or in pairs—pretty typical behavior for wolves with young in summer. In mid-June, the pack moved to a rendezvous site south of its den, and then in July, the wolves left the Absaroka-Beartooth Wilderness, heading south back into the park where they remained through early winter. Beginning in September, when the lone pup was fully capable of traveling with his packmates, the Soda Butte pack was almost always together.

Besides #2 dispersing, three more wolves dispersed. Wolf #8 left the Crystal Creek Pack in late September and found #9 and her eight pups in the Rose Creek pen in early October before they were released. Fortunately for #8, this was only two days before we were scheduled to release #9 and her pups. After release, #9 paired with #8 who immediately accepted all of the pups as his own. The pair has been living on the western edge of the Lamar Valley and will likely breed in 1996.

Wolf #12 from the Soda Butte Pack left in mid-December 1995, and was found dead in mid-February 1996 at the south end of the greater Yellowstone ecosystem. Cause of death at this writing is unknown.

Wolf #3, from the Crystal Creek Pack, also dispersed in late December 1995. Unfortunately, he traveled to Paradise Valley, an agricultural area north of the park. He visited a facility holding captive wolves on December 26, but then moved to a sheep ranch where he killed two sheep. Policy states that each wolf be given two chances, so #3 was captured and re-released after being held several days in a pen. Wolf #3 liked the sheep ranch and made his way back. He was not welcome there, and this was his second strike. According to the agreed upon plan, #3 had to be removed.

These are the first stories of wolf freedom in Yellowstone. One unexpected aspect of this story that bears mentioning was the wolves' visibility. Much of the wolf reintroduction happened before our eyes and the eyes of thousands of Yellowstone visitors. Approximately 4,000 people observed the Crystal Creek wolves traveling, killing, eating, and sleeping in Lamar Valley. As long as people stayed on the road, the wolves were not bothered. They came to accept people as no threat along the road and carried on normal wolf behavior, uninterested in the large crowds gathering almost daily. The reliable viewing of the wolves was a sensation for park visitors. Visitation at the northeast entrance, the nearest entrance, climbed, as visitation at other entrances sagged. Business at Roosevelt Lodge, a nearby resort, boomed. The visitors to Yellowstone loved the wolves, a strong testimony to how Americans, in general, feel about restoring wolves to the world's first national park. Normally shy and elusive, these special representatives of a whole new wolf history in Yellowstone did what wolves do, in front of adoring park visitors.

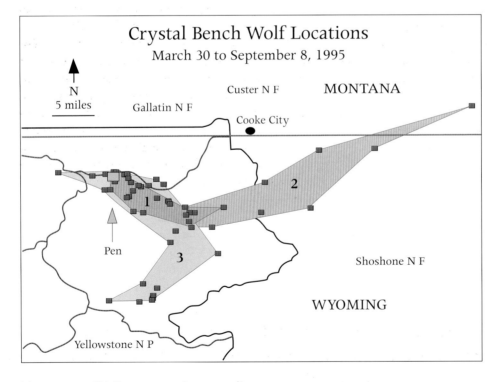

Movements of Yellowstone wolves

Composite range map depicting movements by Yellowstone wolves from March 31 through September 8, 1995. The phrases "Crystal Bench" and "Crystal Creek" were initially used interchangeably; the pack responsible for the movements depicted in the figures is correctly called the Crystal Creek Pack. The period of "post-release" movements is depicted in the range map by the area denoted by the numeral 1. The period of "exploratory movements" is depicted in the range map by the area denoted by the numeral 2. The "settled phase" period is depicted in the range map by the area denoted by the numeral 3. The black line in the range map denotes the boundary of Yellowstone, whereas the red lines denote the road system within the park.

THOUGHTS FROM THE FIELD: WAYNE G. BREWSTER

Wayne G. Brewster is Deputy Director for the Yellowstone Center for Resources. He was the technical committee chairman for the Wolf Management Committee effort in Yellowstone, oversaw preparation of the "Wolves for Yellowstone?" reports, and was the National Park Service representative on the planning team for the Environmental Impact Statement.

There was a clink of metal against metal, a flurry of movement among the shipping containers, and then a gray wolf bounding through the moonlit snow across the Rose Creek pen. The night so still, each lunge in the snow could be heard; the silhouette unmistakable; one of those images that is indelible. We left the pen and started the trek down to the Lamar Ranger Station. The view was like an Ansel Adams masterpiece: white and black clouds, white and black forest, white and black valley floor, lit by a nearly full moon. We paused. No one had done this before; no one would do this again.

It was well after midnight, January 13, 1995, and we were exhausted. We had just finished opening the shipping containers in the Crystal and Rose Creek acclimation pens after a nationally televised drama that included all the elements of a made-for-TV movie—suspense, international intrigue, courtroom drama, and wildlife. The Federal Court order precluding the wolves' release from the small shipping containers was lifted about 6:00 P.M., so we grabbed our equipment and some food and left before someone changed their mind.

Throughout that hectic week, and the previous six months, people put in extraordinary efforts; Canadians and Americans—people from Alberta, British Columbia, Alaska, Montana, Wyoming, Idaho, Minnesota. There were biologists, technicians, veterinarians, and pilots as you would expect. But there were also electricians, carpenters, mechanics, telecommunications specialists, rangers, truck drivers, wranglers, and a whole lot more. They worked together, contributing their skills and talents, and gave 120 percent. Without them, it would not have happened.

The kaleidoscope of memories since I became involved in 1979, seventeen years ago, could be perpetual: the Recovery Plan preparation, the discussions, the congressional briefings, the court appearances, the testimony, the study, the reports, the seemingly endless debate on all the biological, legal, economic, and philosophical nuances. The difference is that was all talk and paper. These were flesh-and-blood wolves, impervious to all our perceptions, and would again do in Yellowstone what wolves do so magnificently— be wolves. The baritones had been returned to Yellowstone's choir; the big dogs were back.

The next generation of rhetoric would focus not on the concept or idea of wolves in Yellowstone, but would now focus on wolves—real wolves. Future generations will judge the wisdom of this endeavor just as this generation has concluded that the extermination of all wolves in the West went too far. Now our children and grandchildren will be able to decide first hand if wolves are important, rather than forevermore being forced to get along without them.

An argument for wilderness that goes deeper still is that we have an ethical obligation to provide animals with a place where they are free from the impingements of civilization.
—Barry Lopez, *Crossing Open Ground*, 1983

Mike Phillips ground-tracking wolves

Unlike other wolf studies, we are able to learn much about the wolves via ground-based radio-tracking.

THOUGHTS FROM THE FIELD: JOHN D. VARLEY

John D. Varley is Director of the Yellowstone Center for Resources. For a decade before, he was Yellowstone's chief of research. John oversees a staff of sixty National Park Service specialists and researchers, and coordinates the efforts of more than 200 scientists working in Yellowstone, including the team monitoring the Yellowstone wolves.

For a whole host of reasons, it was a memorable day. It had all of the makings of a superb TV drama, maybe even as good as a soap opera! The first Yellowstone wolves in sixty years were finally ready to come to the park. They had been captured and kenneled in Canada, and were, as was once said of a famous presidential candidate, "tanned, rested, and ready." The capture had gone pretty well, but the Canadian "greens" were beginning to make a fuss. The sure-thing-can't-miss government transport airplane was delayed, and the pick-up was late. A well-placed rumor had it that a prominent western senator had muscled the U.S. Customs into denying U.S. entry, when the plane made its mandatory landing in Great Falls, Montana. Other opponents were trying to use state and federal animal disease regulations to stop the wolves. Yellowstone's wolves were off-loaded at Great Falls, but the wheeled transport and crew were waiting for them in Missoula. Real drama.

The federal court in Cheyenne, Wyoming, was busy, the opposition forces looking for an injunction to stop the wolves from coming. They did not get that, but they did get a temporary injunction preventing biologists from releasing the wolves from their small transport crates into their commodious acclimation pens. Humane interests were outraged.

Expecting to be ready for any kind of potential trouble, the ranger convoy carrying the wolves were tired after driving here and there across Montana, and being awake for almost twenty-four hours, but their spirits must have lifted when they drove through the Roosevelt Arch and heard the cheers and the applause from the assembled crowd. The seniors from nearby Gardiner High School simply walked out of their classrooms to view the spectacle. Already the most famous wolves in the world, they were met in the shadow of Teddy's arch to the fanfare of the national, regional, and local media, a cabinet secretary, and the director of the nation's primary wildlife agency. The expected protesters apparently decided to stay home and grumble.

In the history of Yellowstone Park it may have been the biggest and most strikingly similar media event to the greater Yellowstone fires of 1988. That's a fairly bold and stunning comparison, because those fires generated the biggest media show in the history of the U.S. national park system. What the two events had in common included a dramatic event, complete with a consortium of high-level government officials, security forces of near presidential intensity, lots of rank-and-file workers scurrying around with determined and solemn faces, hoards of print journalists jockeying around, seeking original stories, and an armada of satellite up-link trucks ready to beam the story to audiences worldwide.

The wolf media center was a gymnasium in Mammoth Hot Springs. When Interior Secretary Bruce Babbitt rose to the podium for his press conference there were twenty-three television cameras pointed at him and nearly 200 other journalists in the audience. It was some show. But why? Was it worth all the trouble? The money? The stress and anxiety? It was indeed. Like the fires of 1988, it may take a century for people to look back on the wolf event and make some meaningful judgments on the ecological and spiritual consequences of what happened in 1995. But for now, we can feel some joy and credit ourselves for having the belated decency to right a long-standing wrong.

Rose Creek pack rendevous

Spotted from an airplane, the Rose Creek Pack rests in the snow, on the loose in Yellowstone.

Kills

It was November 1995, and several inches of snow blanketed Lamar Valley. Even though the growing season was long over, the lush grass from a moist summer still kept the elk fat. Large herds had begun to filter down into the valley, driven there by snow in the high country. Groups of elk, some numbering in the hundreds, could be seen milling about the valley. Abruptly, the calm changed and a group began running, often reversing direction or splitting into separate directions, all the while rapidly re-sorting themselves. As the elk parted, we saw wolves amongst them. The Crystal Creek wolves lived in the Lamar, and the moving herds of elk signaled their return.

On this particular early winter day, we could easily see the wolves and elk from the road. Two black yearlings ran together at the herd, causing it to split into two groups and drawing the attention of a wolf to each. At first each wolf looked casual, running at what appeared to be only half-speed. They seemed to be sifting through the elk as a shepherd would through sheep. Suddenly, one wolf charged ahead at full speed, pressing toward one of the elk. Immediately it was obvious, even to us, that the elk was favoring its right hind leg. The cow, as it ran, looked distinctively different from the other elk running with it; she was not able to fully extend her leg. Quickly, she realized that the wolf was after her, and she attempted to become lost by intermingling with the rest of the herd. But this was to no avail, the wolf was locked in on her like a fighter pilot to a target.

The focus of this chase drew the attention of the other wolf, so now two wolves were pursuing the partly crippled elk. Her efforts to lose herself in the rest of the herd were futile. She turned away and ran alone, trying to outrun the wolves. The threesome was now heading right at us, and even though a mile out into the valley, the intensity of the chase had now overtaken us. Despite her leg, the elk had no intention of giving up, and the wolves still had trouble catching up to her. Once at her side, the wolves wasted no time before they began leaping at the elk's neck, trying to grab hold with their powerful canine teeth. At first, neither wolf could hold on; the elk was still running too fast, and occasionally kicking out with her front legs. One time, a kick knocked a wolf down under her, so she trampled it with her hind legs. The wolf was instantly back to its feet, having lost no ground at all.

Running with two wolves jumping at her side for about a half-mile began to tire the elk. The wolves seemed to sense this, leaping with renewed energy, their bites now taking hold on her neck. The wolves' grip on the elk's neck was so tenacious that they flopped with their whole body against her side for seconds at a time before falling off. But they were right back to grab hold again. After each wolf had dangled from the elk's side several times, she weakened again. Now she was stumbling, falling to the ground, with the wolves on top of her. But she kept fighting to her feet. The wolves kept leaping for new grips onto her neck. One time it appeared that they had her down, but she shook them off and powered to her feet yet again. By now, she was fatally weakened and the wolves knew it, diving in for that last grip on her neck. Finally it came. She went down and did not get up. Five minutes after the chase began, the elk succumbed. The wolves stood over her panting, with mouths agape. They looked around, sniffed her briefly, and did nothing. She was dead. They were alive. There was nothing more. This is what wolves do.

∞

The single most controversial thing about wolves is that they kill. Plain and simple, wolves have to kill to live. Human fascination with this fact is interesting, because

Wolves with elk

By early November, groups of elk, sometimes containing hundreds of individuals, can be seen grazing throughout the Lamar Valley. In 1995, the elk were faced with a new predator with the return of the wolves. Hunting elk, the wolves will often divide groups of elk as they search for individuals upon which to prey.

all life exists because something else dies, and many organisms kill to gain the food they need. But why have wolves been singled out as the evil killers? Devil-dog, cold-blooded, bloodthirsty, ruthless, murderers who kill for the pleasure of it—these are all descriptions used to depict wolves. Is it because wolves kill larger prey, whose remains we see, with whom we can identify? It is very unlike the robin struggling over the worm whose remains and signs of battle are hidden to us. Or is it because wolves kill the animals we husband, our cattle, sheep, and dogs? The myth, hatred, and love of wolves largely stems from how we view their killing.

This is interesting because we are every bit the killer wolves are. We hunt wild game to eat, and so do wolves. This is their problem: Wolves compete with us, and it is for this reason we hate them. To justify our killing, we describe the wolf's killing as cruel and inhumane. Somehow we have come to view our killing as different and better. It is quick and efficient. We do not view our killing as wrong, but every time a wolf kills, it is vicious and bloodthirsty. Yet, this is how death has come to prey for thousands of years, long before we had the efficient means to kill that we now possess. Anything we do is

good and necessary, and in no way cruel. We do not place the same value judgments on ourselves that we do on the wolf, or all predators for that matter.

We need not view wolf killing as anything special. It is a process that deserves no value judgment from us. Since we are part of the natural world, and not separate from it, our penchant to judge is irrelevant. Moral decisions about right or wrong do not apply to the natural world.

We receive letters and comments stating that it is wrong to restore wolves because they are cruel and will "tear an elk apart still alive . . . while screaming in pain" or because we should "leave the peaceful grass eaters alone." First, although this can happen, eating prey alive is rare. Screaming in pain is even less common. Second, it is not our role to determine what kinds of animals we want. People are not the center of the universe; there is other life—life that has functioned for millions of years without our tinkering. Like it or not, it is not our place to determine a creature, or natural process as good or bad. We just have to respect other life forms.

Given this human hatred of wolves, we can ask: Is the world big enough for us to share it with creatures we compete with and don't like? Is wolf restoration appro-

Coyote chasing river otters

The single most controversial thing about predators is that they must kill to survive, plain and simple. For a predator to live, it must kill or scavenge, as with this coyote trying to steal a fish killed by a river otter.

priate in Yellowstone? We feel it is, and firmly believe that the earth does not belong entirely to humans. We do not advocate wolves everywhere, certainly not where we raise our domestic animals; but where humans have a light presence, like the Yellowstone ecosystem, wolves can still exist. They can live as they did before we came to dominate. In fact, we should fight to save a place for wolves to live, not just relegate them to the far north, but work to keep vestiges of wildness separate from humans throughout the world. Indeed, a world without suitable wolf country would be a world not worth inhabiting. Do we want our world to consist only of pavement, plazas, farms, and fields?

Another factor contributing to wolf hatred is the perception of wolves as indiscriminate killers. The belief is that wolves kill whatever they want. This is another wolf myth. Time and again it has been shown that when wolves are hungry, they end up with the easiest target possible. Bringing down large prey is risky business, so risky a wolf can easily be killed by the prey it pursues. Wolves must be selective. In fact, most of the prey they seek to kill, they are not able to fell. Most healthy adult prey are simply too swift or strong for wolves to bring down without

some kind of advantage. Typically, wolves find the weakest, oldest, or youngest members of their prey. Many prey animals killed by wolves have bone deformities or arthritis conditions that predisposes them to wolf predation. These predisposing factors make some animals vulnerable to being killed by wolves, and wolves end up killing these animals. Hence, and contrary to popular myth, wolves are not random killers.

What makes prey vulnerable to wolves is much more complex than age or health; long winters and deep snow can also make prey more vulnerable. Consider, too, that if a mid-winter thaw occurs followed by cold temperatures, it can create a crust on top of the snow on which wolves can walk. Typically, the wolves' prey breaks through the snow's crust. Under these circumstances, wolves have a decided advantage. Understanding these relationships are complex and the subject of current research and lively debate, which through time will modify the details, but not the overall picture of wolf selectivity.

That wolves are selective predators is such a well-established fact that some have suggested that the Yellowstone wolf research project focus on aspects of predator-prey ecology other than wolf prey selectivity.

Changes in elk mortality rates or kill rates (the interval in days between kills) may yield more unique data. Vulnerable prey abounds in Yellowstone, and how the wolves will respond is an exciting question. Fortunately, these pursuits are not mutually exclusive, and we will be able to garner data on both aspects of wolf predation.

WOLVES AS PREDATORS

What can we learn from studying wolf predation? The most important information is to determine species, sex, age, and condition of the prey animal killed. All of this can be easily learned from a skull with teeth, a leg bone,

preferably the femur, and the pelvis and vertebrae. The skull indicates species and sex, the leg bone, with its marrow, can be analyzed for fat content to determine condition, and the vertebrae and pelvis can be checked for bone pathology, such as arthritis—a fairly common malady in hoofed animals. With these data from each wolf kill, and measurement of the interval between kills, we can learn a great deal about predator-prey relationships in Yellowstone.

So far, the Yellowstone wolves have mostly killed elk. Other than elk, we know of two moose and one mountain goat killed by wolves. No bison have been killed.

Battling mule deer bucks
While wolves choose a variety of prey, animals weakened or otherwise predisposed to predation are usually taken. During the rut, males deplete much-needed energy stores, making them especially vulnerable to wolf predation.

The problem for the predator is a different one. His education is elaborate, his preparation extensive. Left to his instincts he would die. He must know his fellow creature much more thoroughly than they know him. He must know which challenges to accept and which to avoid. He must know how to feint with a large and potentially dangerous adversary and see how he hooks his horns. Like the matador, the wolf must study his potential prey and know where to put his body in those critical last seconds before his jaws close on the elk's throat. More than one poor student from a wolf litter has ended up feeding the ravens and other carrion seekers, his side split open, his body mangled by his intended prey.
—Roger Caras, *The Custer Wolf*, 1966

Bison represent one of the wolves' most formidable prey, and a wolf probably needs previous experience with them to be able to take one down. Yellowstone wolves have tested these behemoths, but, more often than not, when wolves chase bison over a hill, they reappear moments later, retreating—with the bison in hot pursuit. This scenario may change, however, as the wolves placed in the Nez Perce pen are experienced with bison.

Of the elk taken, the majority of them have been old cows and calves. Besides being old, three of the forty-three elk kills we have visited had bone deformities. Two of these elk had arthritis in the hip, and another's joint was so deteriorated it was difficult for the animal to run.

These kills do much more than provide food for wolves. Almost the minute the chase is over, scavenging birds swoop in to steal a morsel of meat. Ravens and magpies visit every kill, as do golden and bald eagles. The birds provide good guides to the field kills when we travel to collect them.

Coyotes move in soon after the wolves begin feeding. The coyotes keep their distance, though, as wolves will kill a coyote if it gets too close. Nonetheless, if a wolf walks a hundred yards away to bed down, coyotes will quickly move in for a meal. Risky behavior—and it has

Species and age of prey killed by wolves in Yellowstone National Park from March 1995 through December 1995.

Species	Calves Killed	Adults Killed	Old Adults Killed	Total Killed
Elk	12	19	9	40
Moose	0	0	2	2
Mtn. Goat	0	1	0	1
Deer	0	0	0	0
Bison	0	0	0	0

Number of elk killed during a 25-day intensive monitoring period from November 1995 through early December 1995.

Pack	Time Period	Total Kills	Species Killed	Kill Interval/Days
Crystal	11/11–12/2	7	Elk	3.6
Rose	11/13–12/7	5	Elk	5

cost a few coyotes their lives. Typically, coyotes and wolves do not get along. Where the two occur, coyotes usually take it on the chin. Wolves that move into coyote populations have been known to greatly reduce or even eliminate coyotes. The summer after the wolves arrived, coyote researchers Jenny Sheldon and Bob Crabtree watched the wolves dig out a coyote den, trying to get to the pups. The coyotes of the Lamar Valley, the area where wolves roamed, had fewer pups than did coyotes in the other areas of Yellowstone where there were no wolves. At this writing, we know of twelve coyotes killed by wolves, but there were likely many more undetected by us, and reports of wolves chasing coyotes are common. Clearly this will be one of the more exciting dramas to observe as wolves take hold in Yellowstone.

WOLVES AND GRIZZLY BEARS

Not all scavengers at wolf kills have to be so careful. Grizzly bears walk right up to a kill and help themselves. Roughly a quarter of the kills made by wolves were visited by grizzly bears, and there were likely more. Bears seem to be the "winners" around a wolf kill. We have only observed one instance when wolves and a grizzly were simultaneously at the same carcass, and the bear had the decided advantage. The Crystal Creek wolves were cautious around this bear, never getting too close, and when the bear whirled around, a wolf walking behind turned and ran. Such encounters are evidence that wolves will likely help grizzly bears in the Yellowstone ecosystem. Bears typically find abundant meat in the spring when elk calves are easy prey. By "winning" at wolf kills,

which occur throughout the year, bears will probably have more meat available to them.

Bears at kills present an interesting situation for us. No one wants to collect a kill that is still being used by a bear. The bears have more of a right to the kill than we do, and we do not want to disturb them, possibly causing abandonment of the carcass. And, just as important, no one wants to walk up to a carcass with a bear on it, because more likely than chasing the bear away is the possibility that the bear will defend its food. To guard against this, we always wait several days before retrieving a kill. This allows all of the scavengers to benefit from the kill without human disturbance. Not that the animals won't come back when we leave, but in the spirit of Yellowstone being a place for animals, we like to collect kills after the ecological community has had its fill at them. Granted, we might lose a bone or two to a coyote or wolverine, but in the long run, this will affect our work precious little. Despite waiting to collect the kills, we still run the risk of bumping into a bear. Extreme care is necessary when approaching a kill at anytime. We always use bear spray and lots of noise so we won't surprise a bear. If a kill is in heavy cover, you will hear us poking around and yelling, "Hey, bear! Hey, bear!"

The wolf kills are a boon to the ecological community of Yellowstone. Wolves provide year-round food for numerous scavengers and smaller predators, alike. All of these other animals evolved with wolves, so having wolves back will only benefit the entire ecological community, not injure it, as some have suggested. As evidence, look at how quickly wolves have once again found their place. It's almost like they never left.

Blood-streaked snow with wolf kill

Soon after release, the Soda Butte Pack killed an elk calf weakened by a long winter. Spotted from an airplane, the pack makes a meal of the calf. (Photo © Douglas Smith, National Park Service)

Mike Phillips, left, and Doug Smith inspecting wolf-killed elk

Winter often leaves prey weak and vulnerable to predation. Wolf #10 probably killed this bull elk that was malnourished because of a long winter. Inspecting such kills yields important information about predator-prey relationships. Oftentimes, we will break open the femur bone to inspect the marrow, which is a good indicator of the health of the animal. (Photo © Douglas Smith, National Park Service)

**Joe Fontaine
with wolf pup**
*Joe Fontaine of the
U.S. Fish and
Wildlife Service
holds one of the
pups born to alpha
female #9, the
first litter born to
a Yellowstone
wolf. The pup is
about three weeks
old and weighs
about five pounds.
(Photo © U.S.
Fish & Wildlife
Service)*

Red Lodge Rescue

*T*he message from Doug was clear: #10 was dead. After hanging up the phone, I stared out the window and wondered about #10.

Strangely enough, I was not surprised by #10's death. I know that there are many local residents who believe the only good wolf is a dead wolf. I had been worried about wolves #9 and #10 ever since I located them two days earlier, within four miles of downtown Red Lodge. I did not like the location because it was so close to town. I knew that wolves that lingered near towns were usually killed.

I was especially worried about #10. He was large, sure of himself, and boldly indifferent toward me and the others that provided him food while he was held in captivity in the Rose Creek pen. This bold indifference was shared by none of the other wolves transported from Canada, and it set #10 apart as a truly unique wolf.

I wished that #9 and #10 had stayed in the remote mountain forests to the west, where game was plentiful. They could have stopped anywhere and never have gone hungry. But I know that wolves are motivated by more than hunger. I suppose that curiosity prompted them to travel from ridge to ridge, always excited by the next horizon.

As I thought about #10's life and death, I was struck by his role in two events, one that is right and one that is wrong. Aldo Leopold wrote, "A thing is right when it tends to preserve the integrity, stability, and beauty of the biotic community. It is wrong when it tends otherwise." As one of the fourteen wolves restored to Yellowstone, #10 was an integral part of a thing that is right. By being senselessly murdered, #10 was an integral part of a thing that is wrong.

The ringing phone ended my daydream and reminded me that I had to contact law enforcement so they could begin the investigation. And there was the

questions about what to do with #9. We were not certain, but we had an inkling that she was about to give birth to a litter of pups. But with #10 gone, she would have no help raising the pups. I wondered if we should return her to Yellowstone. I was worried that her chances of surviving near Red Lodge were no better than #10's.

Clearly, we had a big task before us, and #10 deserved that we do it well.

∞

Probably the same day that wolf #10 was shot, his mate, female #9, gave birth to eight pups. We did not know this immediately, but became suspicious after #9 failed to move for many days. It would be unusual for an adult female wolf to restrict movements during late April unless she was tending a litter of pups.

Our suspicions grew every day that she continued to stay put. To be on the safe side, the decision was made to provide #9 supplemental food. We knew that without a mate she would have to hunt on her own. If pups were present, then #9 would have to leave them unattended to hunt. We thought that if we gave her food, we could reduce the amount of time she spent away from the pups. After a few days, the U.S. Fish and Wildlife Service detailed Joe Fontaine to Red Lodge to monitor #9's movements more closely. While ground tracking on May 4, 1995, Fontaine discovered the den site and the litter. He quickly counted seven pups before making a hasty retreat.

Once we confirmed that #9 had given birth, then a decision had to be made about what to do. Some biologists felt that she and the pups should be left alone. They favored the idea that nature was best suited to decide their fates. In contrast, Doug, myself, and the others believed that the family should be returned to Yellowstone.

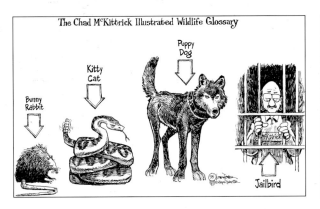

Wolf #10's poacher, Chad McKittrick, later claimed he thought the wolf was a large stray dog. (Cartoon © John Potter, The Billings Gazette)

(Cartoon © John Potter, The Billings Gazette)

Our logic was simple: The den was so close to town that we believed the pups' chances of survival were low. Many folks near Red Lodge do not support the restoration effort, and we were concerned that the closeness of the den would prompt them to take matters into their own hands. Additionally, even if the pups survived to an age of self-sufficiency, we thought it unlikely they would disperse through the rugged mountain country that stood between them and the park. We thought it more likely that they would disperse to the north and east along the front of the mountains. Such movement would place them on private land that was used extensively by livestock, and we thought their chances of surviving in such country was poor.

We believed it was our responsibility to return the family to the safety of the park. Eventually, after many discussions, this belief prevailed. On May 18, Joe Fontaine, Carter Niemeyer, wolf specialist for the Agriculture Department's Animal Damage Control, and Mark Johnson and Doug captured #9 and the pups. The family was immediately transported to the park and placed in the Rose Creek pen, well out of harm's way.

We soon decided the family should be held until the pups were old enough to contribute to their own survival. Yellowstone is a dangerous place for a young wolf, and we knew that without a mate to help provide food, #9 would have to leave the pups unattended for extended periods of time to hunt. We wanted the pups mature enough to fend for themselves in her absence. Accordingly, we decided to release the family in mid-October 1995, when the pups would weigh about fifty pounds.

While #9 settled into a routine of quiet acceptance of confinement, the pups grew like weeds. When captured on May 18, they weighed just five pounds, but by June 26, they weighed almost twenty pounds. Summer was progressing as we expected—at least until Saturday, July 29, when the winds began to blow.

For about fifteen minutes, record-force winds raced through the Rose Creek drainage. The strain on the spruce trees was great and a few toppled to the ground, including two that fell across the pen, creating two large holes. Since Doug and I are based at park headquarters, which is an hour's drive from Rose Creek, we had no knowledge of the disaster until Doug went to the pen to feed the wolves on Monday. He was shocked by the damage and the fact that all eight pups were missing. Only #9 was present, pacing nervously around the inside perimeter.

Doug placed a hasty phone call to me with a status report. I immediately organized a capture crew. We left headquarters not sure what we were going to do, but certain we had to do something.

The crew consisted of Doug, me, and two others, all on horseback. We split ranks and established observation points about 400 yards east and west of the pen. Once in position, we sat and watched, hoping to see the pups. We expected them to be nearby, but minutes passed, and we saw nothing. Growing impatient, I decided to howl, hoping to entice the pups to reveal their locations. That was all the cajoling they needed. Not only did they howl, but they came spilling out from under a big Douglas fir, in a mad headlong rush to #9. Three of the pups were so excited that they ran back in the pen through one of the holes! The excitement provided us an opportune time to try to catch the others, so we left our outposts with nets in hand.

We were able to keep the three in the pen, but the other five were quick and they easily avoided capture. I remember chasing #17, the small gray female. I was running quietly, not far behind, certain that I was gaining on her with every step. I thought she should be able to run faster. Maybe it was the uphill grade that was slowing her, as it was certainly having that effect on me. As I began to tire, I prepared to lunge with my net. In my

Requiem for alpha male #10
The war on the wolf was supposed to be over, but the murder of #10 indicated otherwise.

mind's eye, I saw the net falling over her head, wrapping her up safely and securely. Just then, she turned her head slightly and looked me in the eye. Instantly, her pace quickened, while mine continued to slow. I readied the net thinking that success was a second or two away. Then I tripped.

I like to think that ten years earlier I could have easily caught #17. But ten years is a long time, and I had grown slow and clumsy.

We repaired the pen and captured two more of the pups. As we continued with capture efforts, we established an observation post that allowed us to observe the habits and abilities of the three free-ranging pups without being detected. It soon became apparent that the pups did not need to be captured. We learned that the pups never wandered more that a few hundred yards from the pen. Strong social bonds to #9 and their siblings held them secure to the area. We realized that even though they were not captive, they really had not been

released. One evening we watched them fend off two coyotes that seemed intent on displacing them from the area or killing them. After that, we felt much better about their abilities to survive the dangers of Yellowstone. We terminated capture attempts, continued to leave food outside the pen, and accepted that the family would not be reunited until we opened the gate in mid-October.

On October 9, we went to the pen to administer vaccinations and outfit each pup with a radio-collar. As we processed the animals, we realized that six pups were present, not five. Apparently, some time during the last few days, one of the three pups outside the pen simply could not stand the separation any longer, and climbed in from the outside. While the pens are designed to prevent *escapes* by climbing, apparently they can be *entered* by climbing.

We released the family two days later. At that time, the two remaining pups were in the vicinity of the pen along with, much to our surprise, a young male known

Capture of #9

U.S. Fish and Wildlife Service employee Joe Fontaine, left, and National Park Service employee Mark Johnson tend to wolf #9 after she was captured near Red Lodge, Montana. Wolf #9 was the mate to #10, and after his death, she gave birth to eight pups. Wolf #9's den site was close to Red Lodge, where her and the pups' survival was in doubt. She and the pups were captured and returned to the safety of Yellowstone park. (Photo © Douglas Smith, National Park Service)

as #8. We surmised that #8 had just dispersed from the Crystal Creek Pack and wandered into the Rose Creek drainage. On the day of release, filmmaker Ray Paunovich observed the two free pups begging food from #8's mouth. We were understandably excited by #8's presence. Before stepping outside the pen, #9 already had a suitor.

The Rose Creek Pack has done well since release. They have limited movements to the park and been successful killing prey. We have seen the pack on a number of occasions, and we know that the pups and #8 have developed strong social bonds. And #9 is obviously pleased by #8's presence, or she would not have allowed him to remain with the pack. Only one unfortunate incident has occurred. During the evening of December 20, 1995, pup #22 was hit and killed by a vehicle. We expect the Rose Creek Pack to winter well and produce pups in spring 1996.

THE FATE OF THE WOLVES

The Red Lodge rescue and subsequent events illustrate the importance of individual animals at the beginning of a restoration program. In this respect, restoration differs from traditional wildlife biology, where the principal focus of work is the population rather than the individual animals. At the time #9 gave birth to the eight pups, there were only twelve other wolves in the Yellowstone ecosystem. The Rose Creek family thus comprised 43 percent of the population. It seemed only prudent to do whatever we could to ensure their welfare.

If we are successful, with time our focus will shift from the individuals to the population. A good example of how this shift occurs comes from the red wolf restoration program. At the beginning of the Alligator River project, when the population consisted of just a few wolves, we imple-

mented a prophylactic parasite control program. Because each wolf was valuable, we wanted to reduce the magnitude of the chronic problems caused by parasites. Each month we would inject a broad-spectrum parasiticide into a piece of meat that we placed where a wolf was sure to find and ingest it. This prophylactic program worked well, and we were able to minimize the effect of parasitism.

As the red wolf population grew, two things happened. First, it became difficult for us to implement this parasite control program because of the time required to provide the medicine to a large number of wolves. Second, as the population grew, individuals became less important to the population's persistence.

It will be a few years before we can begin to ignore the fate of individual wolves in Yellowstone. But, if we are successful, the population will grow, and our management of individuals will become less specific and less intense.

We were criticized by some who felt that #9 and her pups should be left alone. These folks argued that nature should be allowed to follow its own course and decide the fate of the family. They argued that it was heavy-handed and unnatural for us to return the family to Yellowstone. They felt we were responding to the emotion of the moment and making a management decision based on a specific issue, rather than a program-wide consideration.

Their arguments confused me. Restoration is by definition heavy-handed, issue-driven management. And once you accept the importance of individual animals, you realize the decision was rooted in an important program-wide consideration: the welfare of individual wolves.

It would have been easy to say that it was neither our right nor our responsibility to decide the future of the family. We could easily have followed the path defined by

Joe Fontaine works for the U.S. Fish and Wildlife Service as the Project Leader for gray wolf recovery in Montana. In this role, Joe is instrumental in managing wolf recovery in the Montana portion of the Yellowstone ecosystem.

As I drove up the steep road through the spring snow toward the Geology Institute, I wondered whether I would be able to locate wolf #9. Her mate, #10, had been illegally killed several days earlier, and #9's movements had become localized on the north slope of Mount Maurice just outside of Red Lodge, Montana, possibly indicating that she had denned. After a slow and tedious climb, I finally four-wheeled it to the top near the Institute buildings; obviously I was the first person up there that spring. Grabbing the radio receiver and antenna, I started toward the area where #9 had been previously located. My mind wandered back to the previous week when my efforts to locate her from the bottom of the drainage were hampered by a raging spring snowstorm and waist-deep snow.

Reaching the edge of the basin through calf-high snow, I turned on the receiver and immediately heard the female's signal as I slowly descended the slope to an old logging road. While doing this, the Beatles song "Number 9" from the White Album kept going through my head: number 9, number 9. Locating the female's signal while walking down the road was a quiet way to determine her location. After a short distance, I suddenly realized the female was below and somewhat behind me. I started to walk quietly down the hill with the receiver set at the lowest volume, while looking for movement and dirty wolf tracks in the snow, which would indicate a possible den. After about fifty yards, a fresh set of tracks appeared, paralleling the slope, but with no indication of dirt. Continuing, I discovered a day bed and approached to investigate.

Suddenly I heard a noise, almost a squeal. Approaching the area, I could hear whimpering, and, suddenly, the direction of the signal changed dramatically. I quickly looked around for a mound of dirt, some fresh excavation, and realized the whimpering was coming from under a spruce tree. After taking a couple of steps, I lifted a spruce bough and was delighted to see a squirming wiggling mass of seven, maybe eight, wolf pups in a shallow depression lined with duff. The pups' overall appearances and closed eyes indicated that they were four to seven days old. One of the pups definitely stood out from the rest, since it had a golden brown head, whereas all the others were a charcoal-gray color.

I quickly retraced my tracks to the edge of the basin so as not to disturb the pups further. In trying to locate the den, I had come closer to the pups and the female than intended. I immediately took a bearing on #9 and estimated her location as some 200 yards up the slope from the pups. I waited nervously for about ten minutes, hoping my intrusion had not frightened her so much that she would not return. I quietly waited until her signal came from the direction of the pups under the spruce tree. I retraced my tracks back to the pickup, put away my equipment, and started to head back down. In my excitement I buried the pickup in a snow bank and ended up spending two hours digging it out. Such is the life of a field biologist.

A decision was made to capture the female and her pups and return them to Yellowstone National Park. Two weeks later, #9 and her pups, all eight of them, were captured and returned to Yellowstone National Park. While in an acclimation pen, they were provided with food and water until October, when they were released back into the wild. The female and pups remained together after being released and were immediately joined by #8, a male wolf from the Crystal Bench Pack.

To say that I was elated about the discovery of the pups is an understatement. I wanted to yell to the whole world that #9 had produced the first litter of wolf pups in the Yellowstone ecosystem in sixty years, but there was only me, the pups, and the silence of the forest. The reintroduction had worked, and worked well. This was the fruit of twenty-five years of effort by a host of dedicated people to return the wolf back to the ecosystem. I felt humble and proud to be a part of that team, a team that has just won a championship game in wildlife management.

Black wolf pups
At the time of their return to Yellowstone, #9's pups were about three weeks old and weighed about five pounds. (Photo © Douglas Smith, National Park Service)

a laissez-faire attitude. Such a direction was certainly tempting, because we knew that capturing #9 and the pups was a high-stakes operation. Even the best of plans come with the chance that something will go wrong, and we knew that our capture plan was no exception. We knew that once #9 was captured, finding the den could prove difficult. And we knew that if we could not find the den, then we would have to release #9; the pups would not survive long without her. If we had to re-release her, #9 would probably move the pups. The move would expose them to the elements, which could lead to mortalities. We knew that we had no room for error. And if we erred, we knew that we would be severely criticized.

Sometimes the right path is not the easiest. A laissez-faire attitude concerning #9 and the pups was simply wrong. The wolves deserved that we overcome the challenges of capture and bring them home. It was the only responsible thing to do. And we did it.

High-stakes operations are important. The best field crews look forward to such operations because they represent tremendous opportunities to establish credibility. I would never have wished a murderous fate on #10, but his death created a controversial management issue, and in doing so, provided us a great opportunity to establish credibility.

Much of the criticism directed at the wolf restoration project has been based on supposition. People supposed the wolves would kill all the livestock in the area; they supposed that large tracts of public land would be closed to promote wolf conservation; and they supposed that the field crews would not perform credibly. Since there were no wolves or field crews to show opponents differently, suppositions were common, extreme, and accepted.

Wolf #10's death gave us the opportunity to show people—opponents and supporters, alike—our mettle. In that respect, the restoration effort needed a Red Lodge rescue. It gave us the opportunity to establish credibility. After the rescue at Red Lodge, people no longer had to suppose that the federal biologists responsible for the restoration program would perform poorly.

I know that no matter how well we do our jobs, some people will still oppose the restoration effort. I cannot change their minds, and I know that in the final analysis they will say, "I never supported the program, never considered it anything more than a waste of taxpayer's money."

I hope, however, with their next breath they will add, "But you know, those fellows from the park, and the Fish and Wildlife Service, and ADC sure did their jobs well."

That is the essence of the Red Lodge rescue: a job well done.

Growing pup

The wolf pups quickly learned the social skills necessary for their survival. Here, female pup #17 watches warily from the safety of a fallen tree.

Escaped pups

On July 29, 1995, record-force winds raced through the Rose Creek drainage. The storm uprooted two large spruce trees that fell across the pen, creating two large holes. All eight pups escaped. But after escaping, the pups didn't wander more than a few hundred yards from the pen. Strong social bonds to #9 kept them securely rooted to the area.

Wolf pup #23

*After being rescued from Red Lodge, the pups grew like weeds in the Rose
Creek pen. After just one and one-half months, the pups had quadrupled
their weight and now tipped the scales at twenty pounds. Even at ten
weeks of age, the pups, like their mother #9, were very wary of us and
would run and hide when we brought food to the pen.*

Above: **Netting wolf pup #23**

When we were ready to release the pups, we first wanted to collar them. Salmon nets are used to capture the captive wolves so that immobilizing drugs can be easily administered. National Park Service veterinarian Mark Johnson, right, snares the running male wolf pup #23 in his net. Doug Smith, right, then adds a second net to secure the pup. The duo restrain and administer immobilizing drugs to the pup.

Right: **Carrying wolf pup #23**

Once the drug has taken effect, wolves can be easily handled. Mark Johnson, left, and renowned wolf biologist Rolf O. Peterson carry #23 across the pen to the processing area.

Right: **Preparing radio collars**

Mike Phillips, left, and Doug Smith prepare the collars for the pups in the Rose Creek pen prior to their release. Each pup was outfitted with a radio collar that allows us to monitor movements and survival of individuals. Each radio collar transmits a unique signal that allows us to track the individual animal.

Below: **Preparing wolf pups for release**

Prior to release in October 1995, six of the eight Rose Creek pups received a thorough health exam during which we administered vaccinations, drew blood for disease testing, and assessed their overall condition. All were in excellent health. Many different individuals helped with the operation: here, clockwise from left, Doug Smith, Mark Johnson, Yellowstone Photographer Jim Peaco, and volunteer Carrie Schaeffer, are processing female pup #17.

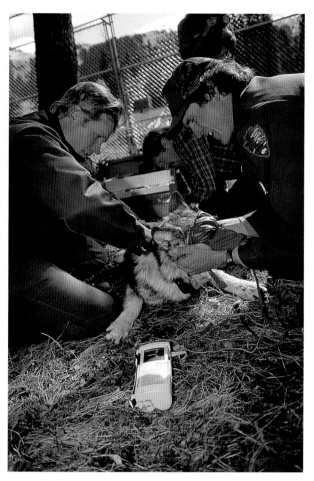

Left: **Readying a pup for release**

Mike Phillips, left, Rolf O. Peterson, center, and Doug Smith process female pup #17. In the foreground is a pulse oximeter that measures respiration rate and other vital signs. Throughout the exams, vital signs were carefully monitored to ensure the welfare of each wolf.

Below: **Release of male pup #21**

Two days after processing, wolf #9 and the six pups were released from the Rose Creek pen.

Wolf #8 standing behind Rose Creek pen

As fate would have it, one day before #9 and the pups exited the pen, wolf #8, who had recently dispersed from the Crystal Creek Pack, arrived in the Rose Creek drainage. We were completely surprised and overjoyed by his presence. If #9 approved of him, it meant that she would have help providing for the eight pups and a mate for the 1996 breeding season.

Three black pups and #8 in sage meadow

Since #8 joined the Rose Creek family, we have seen them on a number of occasions. We know that #8 and the pups have developed strong social ties. And in February, #8 and #9 were observed breeding.

Still the question recurs, "Can we do better?" The dogmas of the quiet past, are inadequate for the stormy present. The occasion is piled high with difficulty, and we must rise with the occasion. As our case is new, so we must think anew, and act anew.

—Abraham Lincoln, address to Congress, 1862

Weighing wolf pups

Doug Smith, right, and Wayne Brewster, Deputy Director Yellowstone Center for Resources, weigh one of the Rose Creek pups. Each pup weighed between fifty pounds to sixty pounds upon release in October 1995.

**Wolf #3 in
capture net**

*Male wolf #3 was
killed on January
25, 1996. He had
become a chronic
problem and he had
to go. I remembered
our promise to the
ranchers and our
credibility was at
stake. I thought
back to when I
watched his eyes in
the capture net in
the pen before the
immobilizing drugs
took affect. They
were filled with
such life and
emotion. I hoped
then that he would
make the best of his
second chance. He
did not. Little did
we know that would
be the last day we
saw #3 alive.*

Incident at Dry Creek

*I*n some respects, the Dry Creek incident began on March 30, 1995, the first day wolf #3 stepped outside the Crystal Creek pen.

Wolf #3 was a member of the Crystal Creek Pack. At the time of release, he was a coal-black pup that stood two and one-half feet tall and weighed eighty pounds. Like his three brothers, #3 had a youthful demeanor. None was old enough to be a serious wolf. But by the time summer turned to fall, the pups had matured into capable predators, and commonly led the hunts.

From the time of his release until December 1995, #3 was always with the pack. Although his brother, #8, left the group during October to start his own pack, #3 did not show signs of wanderlust until December; we last located him with the pack on December 21.

During the next week, we searched from the air and the ground for #3 without success. At about this same time, we received a photograph of a black canid that was frequenting a colony of captive wolves that lived on private property along Dry Creek, about twenty-five miles north of Yellowstone Park and about fifty air miles from #3's last location. While Doug and I found the photograph intriguing, we could only confirm that it was a picture of a black canid. We had no reason to suspect that it was #3. In retrospect, we should have been more suspicious.

On Thursday, January 11, 1996, Horus and Susan Brailsford, ranchers who raise sheep along Dry Creek, reported seeing a wolf and missing one sheep. By midafternoon, Jim Hoover, a regional supervisor for the Agriculture Department's Animal Damage Control Program (ADC), was on site investigating the report. ADC is the federal agency responsible for investigating and managing wolf-livestock incidents. Hoover called at 5:00 P.M. and told me that #3 was in the Dry Creek

drainage, not a stone's throw from the Brailsfords' ranch. Later that evening, Doug and I met Hoover and confirmed #3's location.

The next day, Hoover found the partially eaten remains of a ewe lamb. The autopsy indicted #3 was the culprit responsible for the sheep's death.

Before wolves were ever released, ranchers in the area had vehemently objected to the restoration effort because they feared that it would lead to excessive wolf-induced losses of livestock. And they said they could not afford any losses, especially excessive ones.

To assuage their fears, the federal government promised that wolf-induced depredations would not be tolerated. Ranchers were told that wolves that killed livestock would be quickly and effectively managed to stop the killing. Conservationists who strongly supported wolf restoration grudgingly accepted this promise, which was necessary to ensure success.

Wolf #3 was the first animal to test our resolve and ability to uphold that promise. We knew that ranchers and conservationists throughout the ecosystem would be watching to see how we managed the Dry Creek incident. It was a watershed event. There was no room for error, and no time to blink.

It was clear that #3 had to be moved. There simply was no other choice. The U.S. Fish and Wildlife Service and the National Park Service requested that ADC capture #3. Two days later, this was accomplished using a net fired from a helicopter.

∽

While wolf #3 was creating havoc in Dry Creek, the Soda Butte Pack was causing emotions to stir in communities like Nye and Fishtail, Montana. Starting in early December 1995, the Soda Butte Pack began utilizing public and private land along the front of the Beartooth Mountains

The question of the next century will not be how to save the wolf, but rather how best to manage the animal.

—L. David Mech, "The Challenge and Opportunity of Recovering Wolf Populations," 1995

Above: **Black wolf #3**

At the time of release, wolf #3 was a black pup weighing eighty pounds and standing about two and one-half feet tall. As summer turned to fall, #3's youthful demeanor changed, and by mid-December he had left the pack.

Above: **Wolf #3 traveling through deep snow**

After #3 dispersed, the Crystal Creek Pack included just four wolves: the alpha pair, #4 and #5, and two yearling males, #2 and #6. These wolves continued to restrict movements to their established territory in the Lamar Valley. After dispersing from the Crystal Creek Pack, #3's wide-ranging travels led him to Dry Creek, about twenty-five miles north of Yellowstone park and about fifty miles from the Lamar Valley.

in the northeastern corner of the Yellowstone ecosystem. In contrast to #3, however, the Soda Butte wolves were model citizens. The only incident precipitated by their presence occurred on December 8 and involved a lion hound they killed after the dog followed their trail and tracked them down. The death of the hound was unfortunate, but it would have been inappropriate to blame the wolves for the dog's persistence that led to its death.

Residents of the area, nonetheless, were outraged over the lack of notification that the wolves were in the area, and were concerned that other incidents would arise. They demanded that the pack be moved. We would have notified residents if we had known wolves were in the area, but the 1995–1996 U.S. government shutdown and bad weather had prevented us from keeping close tabs on the wolves.

Within the week, residents had convinced Montana Senator Max Baucus that their demand was valid. Baucus wrote the U.S. Fish and Wildlife Service and echoed the residents' sentiment: return the wolves to the park. Dwight MacKay, a local rancher running for election to the U.S. House of Representatives, also expressed concern, as did Montana Senator Conrad Burns. The U.S. Fish and Wildlife Service responded that the mere presence of the wolves was not justification for their removal.

I was pleased with the Wildlife Service's response. I know from personal experience with the red wolf program the difficulties that arise when wolves are routinely removed from private property in the absence of problems. When the red wolf program was developed during the mid-1980s, high-ranking officials with the U.S. Fish and Wildlife Service promised local citizens that wolves would be captured anytime they wandered outside the refuge's boundaries. I and other members of the field crew reiterated this promise at countless public meetings. As the wolf population grew, upholding that promise became increasingly difficult. Eventually, it nearly destroyed that restoration effort.

Removing wolves from large tracts of private land in the Yellowstone ecosystem in the absence of problems would also be a no-win situation. If we are successful in this restoration effort, some wolves will inhabit private land, while others will travel across it. It is possible that the demand to move wolves could become great enough to consume the project. And for what reason? Simply because the wolves are present?

In the presence of a problem, like the one created by #3, wolves will be moved. That is a certainty. But in the absence of a problem, moving wolves makes no sense and establishes a precedent that could be effectively used to argue for the removal of other endangered species, ranging from grizzly bears to red-cockade woodpeckers, that sometimes inhabit private land. And once this starts, where does it stop?

In the United States, landowners do not own the wildlife that inhabits their property; rather, wildlife are owned by the public. As President Theodore Roosevelt wrote: "Every man holds his property subject to the general right of the community to regulate its use to whatever degree the public welfare may require it."

Within limits, citizens can manage private land in a manner that promotes or hinders the welfare of wildlife. But citizens cannot capture and remove or kill wildlife that inhabit private property, regardless of whether the animals are naturally occurring or present because of a restoration program. This applies to robins, rabbits, elk, and all other wildlife—including wolves. Through local, regional, and national laws enforced by state and federal officers, citizens decide under what circumstances wildlife can be captured and moved or killed. Such decisions are not the prerogative of the individual landowner.

A SECOND CHANCE

The day #3 was captured in Dry Creek we only knew for certain that we wanted to give him a second chance. The rules allowed us to make that choice, and our collective conscience desired it. We placed #3 in the Rose Creek pen and began planning his release.

Since the 1996 Canadian capture and translocation operation was underway, we gave serious thought to placing a female in the pen with #3 and holding them in captivity until late March 1996. As appealing as that scenario was, we were concerned that a female might follow #3 to Dry Creek if he chose to return to the Brailsfords' ranch. Rather than risk a valuable female, we decided to immediately release #3 in the center of Yellowstone, about sixty air miles south of Dry Creek. We did this on January 25, with the hope that #3 would make good use of his second chance and remain within the protective confines of the park.

During the next week, #3 traveled north, and by February 1, he was twenty-eight miles from the release site. Although Doug and I were pleased that he was still in the park, his progress and location made us nervous. He was already halfway back to Dry Creek, and in the bottom of the Yellowstone River drainage that led directly to the Brailsfords' ranch. Our nervousness prompted us to schedule a telemetry flight for the next day. It proved to be a good decision.

The next day was Friday, and by late afternoon, we had located #3 only ten miles from Dry Creek. As we feared, he had followed the Yellowstone River out of the park. He seemed to be on a collision course with disaster.

Capturing wolf #3

After being removed from Dry Creek, #3 was placed in the Rose Creek pen for two weeks in the hopes of re-acclimating him. When the two weeks were up, we had to capture him to ready him for his second release. Capturing a ninety-pound wolf is not an easy task, as Doug Smith shows here. Using a large salmon net, Doug catches #3 as he runs by at full speed. Caught, wolf #3 tumbles over and tries to pull the net from Doug's hands, running straight back at Doug. Mike Phillips quickly places a second, restraining net over wolf #3.

111

Late that night or early Saturday morning, one of the Brailsfords' sheep was attacked. By mid-morning, we located #3 within 200 yards of the Brailsfords' barnyard. Jim Hoover informed the Brailsfords of #3's whereabouts, and they readily agreed to keep their sheep in the barn, out of harm's way.

Wolf #3 had become a chronic problem and he had to go, as certainly this time as the first time. The future of the restoration program depended on it. By late afternoon, the U.S. Fish and Wildlife Service and the National Park Service had requested that ADC remove #3 from the program.

REMOVING WOLF #3

Some events remind us that the more things change, the more they stay the same. Although I had left the Alligator River National Wildlife Refuge to work in Yellowstone, the incident at Dry Creek reminded me of numerous incidents I was involved in while working with red wolves. I remember writing in the journal *Endangered Species Update* after resolving an especially contentious situation that "unlike most endangered species, recovery of the red wolf is not so much dependent on the setting aside of undisturbed habitat as it is on overcoming the political and logistical obstacles to human coexistence with wild wolves." Wolf #3 reminded me that the same would apply to wolf restoration in Yellowstone. That night, the Brailsfords watched from their living room as #3 wandered about the barnyard and investigated the guard dogs who quietly submitted to his large presence.

Everything was happening so quickly that we had no time to place #3 in captivity at an appropriate facility; all of Yellowstone's pens were full of wolves recently shipped from Canada, and there was no place where we could responsibly re-release #3. Out of options, we decided that #3 would have to be killed. ADC began making appropriate arrangements.

Sunday morning brought bad weather that forced ADC to cancel the removal operation. That night the Brailsfords again watched #3 as he milled about the barnyard. When he began chasing the horses, Mr. Brailsford could stand it no longer. He chased #3 from the ranch with a pitchfork. Our resolve strengthened.

There was a light breeze the next morning, but nothing more. Wolf #3 was where we expected he would be: in the bottoms of Dry Creek, not far from the barnyard. While waiting for the helicopter to arrive, we visited with the Brailsfords. They were nice people. They were animal people. Doug and I counted six dogs, at least two

cats, and six horses including two colts. We did not see the sheep because they were still in the barn. The Brailsfords told us they owned about thirty sheep, including the one that had been attacked, which they were nursing back to health.

We apologized for any inconvenience caused by #3. They said they understood. They were not happy with the course of events, and wished that #3 had stayed in the park. They appreciated the compensation they received for the damage caused by #3 when he initially settled in the area, but thought that the Defenders of Wildlife should have provided more money. They did not wish any harm on #3, but agreed that he had to go.

Hoover climbed into the helicopter at 9:45 A.M., and the operation began at 9:49 A.M. At 9:53 A.M., #3 flushed from the creek bottoms, bothered by the sound of the helicopter. At 9:55 A.M., he was shot. Hoover reported that #3 died nearly instantly.

We will never know why #3 returned to Dry Creek. What we do know is that #3 had many choices, and he went back to the Brailsfords'. That decision seemed deliberate. Maybe he was lonely and received social reinforcement from the wolves in the captive colony and the guard dogs at the ranch. Maybe he was attracted to the sheep that were easy to kill. Maybe it was all of these variables acting together. We know that the Brailsfords and their neighbors operate clean ranches; there were no carcass piles to attract #3.

MANAGING THE YELLOWSTONE WOLVES

There is no doubt that conflicts with humans will increase as wolves are restored to areas. Wolf #3 is the first Yellowstone wolf to kill livestock, but he will not be the last. As conflicts increase, it is possible that public backlash will be so strong that management practices will be enacted to once again significantly reduce wolf numbers. Thinking about the Dry Creek incident leads me to wonder how problems can be managed so that the wolf can be restored to as many places as possible.

Many have tried to manage wolf-related problems using nonlethal methods. Unfortunately, most have proven uneconomical, while others, like the Brailsfords' guard dogs, were simply ineffective.

Economic compensation programs, like the one administered by Defenders of Wildlife, minimize public animosity toward wolves, but do nothing to prevent repeat wolf offenses.

Some have suggested that "management zoning" could allow wolves to inhabit areas where they feed on

Facing page: **Carrying drugged wolf #3**
After immobilizing the wolf, Doug Smith, left, and Mike Phillips carry #3 out of the Rose Creek pen to transport him to the release site.

Wolf #3 in shipping kennel
In order to transport #3 from the remote Rose Creek pen to the release site, Mike Phillips and Doug Smith loaded #3 on a sled and then pulled the sled for a mile to the trailhead and a waiting truck. After being transported from the Rose Creek pen, #3 was placed in a shipping crate for transport to the release site.

Second release of wolf #3

After two weeks in captivity, the decision was made to provide #3 a second chance by releasing him in the central portion of Yellowstone, about sixty air miles south of Dry Creek. We did this on January 25, with the hope that #3 would make good use of the second chance and remain within the protective confines of the park. It was not to be.

natural prey, while prohibiting wolves from areas where conflicts with humans are likely. Zoning has an intuitive appeal, and has been applied on a large scale in wolf-recovery planning. But zoning is, at best, only part of a wolf conservation strategy. One must still decide how to manage the wolf that settles in a no-wolf zone, like the Brailsfords' barnyard.

In an article entitled "The Challenge and Opportunity of Recovering Wolf Populations" published in the noted journal *Conservation Biology*, prominent wolf biologist David Mech reviewed several issues relevant to wolf management. He concluded that "Direct lethal control is still usually the only practical course under most conditions. . . . Public education programs must include the message that any restoration of wolves will ultimately result in a need to control them. . . . Thus, if wolf advocates could accept effective control, wolves could live in far more places."

This conclusion was also reached by the designers of the Yellowstone project. As I pointed out in chapter 2, the final rule that governs management of Yellowstone's wolves states: "All chronic problem wolves will be removed from the wild (killed or placed in captivity)." It can be no other way. Local acceptance—or at the least, tolerance—is critical to success and dependent upon this.

Wolf #3 had become a chronic problem. He had to be removed from the population. The future of the restoration effort depended on it. As tragic as it might be, #3's death helped us ensure a future for the other wolves that call Yellowstone home.

Black wolf pup
Yellowstone historian Paul Schullery said it best: "Maybe 120 years from now, Yellowstone managers will be able to look back on this project and make some meaningful judgements on the ecological and spiritual consequences of what we've done today. For the moment, all we can do is give ourselves a little credit for having the belated decency to right such a long-standing wrong and pray for puppies."

Into the Future

That fateful evening probably seemed different to the moose. It was probably not so much because of the grizzly that had been in the area for the last few days. Almost surely the moose had contact with the large boar every spring for over ten years, as they both were probably born in the Pebble Creek drainage. I imagine the two had come to respect one another as the aged in a world where many of their kind do not survive to be elderly. I do not believe the grizzly caused the moose to survey the surroundings a little longer and more often during that fateful evening. It was probably something else, maybe a scent on the wind or a shadow in the forest.

I imagine that the end came swiftly for the moose, because although it had wintered well in the shallow snow under the firs and spruce, it was old and probably not as sure-footed as it once had been. And there were five of them. Five of them that were quick and hungry and cooperative. Five of them each with a keen ability to kill. They were five wolves that were known to me as the Soda Butte group, and they killed the moose.

The wolves fed on the moose extensively, as did the old grizzly. Indeed, Doug and I could not tell who ate the most—the wolves or the bear. I first saw the kill while locating the wolves during a telemetry flight. But Doug found the kill by following grizzly tracks to the site. I suppose it does not matter who ate the most. The wolves had made five kills during the days before encountering the moose, and surely made more after killing it. They were not going hungry. And the old bear obviously knew how to find food.

The moose probably knew something was different on that fateful night. How could it not know? After an absence that spanned almost six decades, one of the most important evolutionary engineers was once again at work in Yellowstone. I suppose the significance of the wolves' return was lost on the moose. It probably would have preferred to have been left alone to eat more willows and worry about the bear.

∞

Wolf restoration began as a dream, and if we are successful it will always be a dream. Not just a dream of wolves living free in a wild place, but rather a dream about the way the world should be, a dream about a new way of thinking that says that to protect human life all life must be protected; to protect human health all life must be healthy. Albert Einstein said, "We cannot solve the problems we have created with the same thinking that created them." Wolf restoration is evidence of a new way of thinking that will lead to protection of ecosystems, biological diversity, and humankind.

Wolves in the Yellowstone ecosystem have a bright future if we are prepared to expect the unexpected. Wolf #10's death and the birth of eight pups within a few miles of Red Lodge illustrate the chaotic, unpredictable side of restoration. Nonetheless, I am optimistic about the future, because I know that our restoration plan will allow us to respond to whatever arises.

In December 1994, no wolves inhabited Yellowstone. As I write this in February 1996, just fourteen months later, the park is home to nineteen free-ranging wolves and seventeen captive wolves that are being prepared for release. The free-ranging wolves are members of four packs, all of which should produce pups in spring 1996. The captive wolves will be released during late March and April 1996. It is entirely conceivable that fifty wolves will lay claim to Yellowstone and its environs by Christmas 1996.

Despite our early success, there remains substantial opposition to the project. This opposition combined with significant changes in the political climate in Washington are cause for concern. We may not have adequate congressional support to implement our plan completely. If this occurs, the restoration effort may fail.

Our successes convince me that now is not the time to withhold support. Too much progress has been made for that to be an intelligent option. Withholding support now would be akin to restoring a fine piece of art and never hanging it in a museum. Now is the time to push full-steam ahead. We can restore wolves to their rightful place in the wilderness community of Yellowstone, but not if we are hamstrung by an unsympathetic Congress and an uninvolved public.

Because wolf restoration consists of more than translocation, acclimation, and reintroduction, we need congressional and public support for a few more years to determine the success or failure of the releases and the effects of wolves on other members of Yellowstone's wildlife community. It is during the post-release period that we will have unprecedented opportunities to gain insight into predation, one of nature's great evolutionary forces.

THE DANCE OF LIFE

I was reminded of the power of predation as I watched two wolves from the Crystal Creek pack kill an cow elk. I was mesmerized by the "dance of life" between predator and prey as the elk struggled and tried to escape. Her desire to survive was as strong as the wolves'. But the long winter had left her weak, and, in the end, she lost the struggle. The dance of life between the wolves and the elk reminded me that predation shapes both predator and prey. Elk and deer and moose are what they are due to eons of attendance by wolves. Poet Robinson Jeffers wrote, "What but the wolf's tooth whittled so fine the fleet limbs of the antelope." I believe that Mr. Jeffers could also have written: What but the moose's stubbornness whittled so fine the dogged determination of the wolf.

Predation has fascinated humankind for a long time. In the book Of Wolves and Men, Barry Lopez writes: "Whether wolf and prey act according to some mutual understanding, or whether they only unconsciously participate in a fundamental drama, is something we shall probably never know. All we do know, staring up at the paintings of game animals on the cave walls at Lascaux, is that the belief that there was more to hunting than killing, and that dying was as sacred as living, was not something that one day just fell out of the sky." Insight into the fundamental drama between predator and prey will improve our understanding of the world around us.

Insight, however, will only be realized through long-term, well-conceived studies of wolves and wildlife species affected by wolf restoration. Because Yellowstone staff

and resources are limited, we cannot exploit every learning opportunity presented by the wolf project. Activities concerning other important aspects of wolf restoration must result from collaborative relationships that we develop with biologists outside Yellowstone. Doug and I, with help from many others, identified the following three activities as the focus of the restoration program's post-release period:

First, daily for thirty days in early and late winter, we should conduct telemetry flights, ground-track wolves, and inspect all known wolf kills to document wolf killing rates and prey selectivity by species, age, sex, and condition.

Second, outside the two periods of winter study, we should conduct telemetry flights every fifth day to document seasonal patterns of predatory behavior, location of dens and rendezvous sites, and changes in wolf numbers, pack structure, spatial organization, and distribution in response to prey migration. We should inspect wolf kills opportunistically to document seasonal patterns of prey selectivity by species, age, sex, and condition.

Third, we should establish genetic profiles for all reintroduced and captured wolves. These profiles will allow us to identify and document reproductive success of individuals, determine relatedness among wolves, and develop population estimation procedures based on genetic samples that we recover "passively" (e.g., scats, hair snares) from wolves.

The learning opportunities presented by wolf restoration are similar in magnitude to the opportunities presented by the Yellowstone fires of 1988 about which ecologists John Varley and Paul Schullery wrote in The Greater Yellowstone Ecosystem: Redefining America's Wilderness Heritage, "The biotic communities of the Greater Yellowstone Area have just received a dynamic jolt of prehistoric dimensions. . . . For nature, and for those of us who love nature and find enrichment and inspiration in her workings, opportunity rarely knocks this loudly in Yellowstone."

Doug and I are determined to answer the knock of wolf restoration. We anticipate that the wolf in Yellowstone will be a keystone predator possessing impressive abilities to reshape ungulate populations, with considerable direct and indirect influences that will ripple through the ecosystem. We must document the effects of the restoration effort. The activities outlined above will allow us to do just that. Additionally, the activities will allow the National Park Service to honor various legal obligations, and they will enable and strengthen future partnerships that will lead to long-term studies of other members of Yellowstone's wildlife community.

Mike Phillips and Doug Smith ground-tracking wolves

Insight into the effect of wolf restoration will only be gained through long-term, well-conceived studies of wolves and wildlife species affected by wolf restoration. Because wolves are highly mobile and secretive by nature, radio telemetry will be a important method in our studies.

PAYING THE COSTS OF WOLF RESTORATION

The Yellowstone wolf restoration program costs about $334,000 annually when we are engaged in translocation and acclimation, and will cost about $220,000 annually during the post-release years. Unfortunately, Congress did not provide adequate support during 1995 and 1996, and the Park Service had to reprogram funds to ensure successful years. Since it is likely that congressional support will continue to wane, Park Service reprogramming will probably be necessary in the future. Such reprogramming, however, unfairly affects other important conservation initiatives. "Robbing Peter to pay Paul" is not an acceptable long-term solution to the problem of inadequate congressional support.

Wolf restoration is one of the most important wildlife conservation initiatives in the history of the United States, and the public is keenly interested and overwhelmingly supportive of the project. Because of this and because of waning congressional support, it seems possible and desirable to develop a public-private partnership so the restoration effort is not wholly dependent on federal funding.

Doug and I and other members of Yellowstone's staff have attempted to be responsive to opportunities to privatize the wolf project. Our fund-raising efforts, however, have been reactive and only marginally successful. Accordingly, we are now hoping to add a new member to our team who will act as the Yellowstone wolf recovery fund coordinator. This person will be responsible for maximizing the effectiveness of public–private partnerships to benefit wolves. The recovery fund coordinator will serve the entire nation by ensuring the fiscal health of the Yellowstone wolf project.

Developing a public-private partnership to benefit the wolf project will serve more than simple fiscal needs. If successful, it will become an important lesson to other wildlife conservation programs that need to divorce themselves from the vagaries of federal funding. During a time when many people believe the federal deficit threatens to undermine the vigor of our government, conservationists must find a path to self-sufficiency; the Yellowstone wolf project may help mark such a path.

THE SIGNIFICANCE OF WOLF RESTORATION

Many view Yellowstone National Park as the embodiment of wilderness, a special place where natural processes are allowed to function unfettered from the belief system of the "civilized" world, a place where nature is allowed to follow its own well-worn paths. Without wolves, however, Yellowstone was incomplete. Certain paths, blocked by the ignorance of the past, could not be followed. Fortunately, simply opening the acclimation pens' gates began clearing those paths.

The significance of wolf restoration transcends the boundaries of the park. Wolf restoration in Yellowstone is infinitely more significant than wolves killing a moose in the Pebble Creek drainage, despite what the moose might think. Wolf restoration in Yellowstone illustrates that the Endangered Species Act can be implemented in a manner that is respectful of the needs and concerns of local citizens and that the act can lead to recovery.

This illustration is extremely important because the act is often portrayed as cumbersome legislation that lacks utility and pits the needs of people against the needs of obscure animals. Many contend that the Endangered Species Act simply does not get the job done in a manner that promotes harmony between humans and other life forms. Indeed, this is the basis for the argument to weaken, if not repeal, the act.

Some erroneously believe that the act has halted thousands of federal projects with subsequent losses of millions of dollars of revenue. Between 1987 and 1992, however, the U.S. Fish and Wildlife Service conducted nearly 97,000 Endangered Species Act consultations with other agencies, and only fifty-four resulted in project terminations.

It is also common to criticize the act based on the belief that hundreds, if not thousands, of landowners have been prosecuted for activities in which they engaged. However, a 1994 report by the General Accounting Office indicates that from 1988 through 1993, the U.S. Fish and Wildlife Service obtained injunctive relief only four times to stop or delay activities that would harm endangered species on private land.

Objective reviews of the Endangered Species Act indicate that it does not have to be weakened, and certainly not repealed. It is one of our country's most important legislative shields against threats to humanity because it protects the wondrous diversity of life on earth upon which humankind is utterly dependent. As I consider the need for a strong Endangered Species Act, I am reminded of the words of Dr. E. O. Wilson in *The Diversity of Life*: "Biodiversity is the key to the maintenance of the world as we know it. Unfortunately, a great extinction spasm is upon us, grace of mankind. Earth has at last acquired a force that can break the crucible of evolution. In the world as a whole, extinction rates are already hundreds or thousands of times higher than before the coming of man. The losses cannot be balanced by new evolution in any period of time that has meaning to the human race. Because scientists have yet to put names on most organisms, and because they entertain only a vague idea of how ecosystems work, it is reckless to suppose that Biodiversity can be diminished without threatening humanity itself."

Wolf restoration is a dramatic expression of the goodness and power of the human spirit. Henry David Thoreau wrote, "I know of no more encouraging fact that the unquestionable ability of man to elevate his life by conscious endeavor." I think wolf restoration is one such conscious endeavor that elevates the lives of people. It shows that we respect the rights of other life forms, even when they may cause problems. It shows that we are capable and committed to correcting the mistakes of the past. Wolf restoration is important because it acts as a touchstone for measuring our reverence for what we have inherited from our ancestors and as a touchstone for measuring our concern for the legacy we leave our chil-

dren. And we need touchstones.

Wolf restoration is also important because of its power to reveal important truths. Pioneer conservationist Aldo Leopold observed in *A Sand County Almanac* that "Encounters with nature reveal, not only insights into natural history, but important truths about human nature." Certainly wolf restoration represents an intimate and prolonged encounter with nature, and I have come to believe that it reveals an important truth about humans: That we gain respect for ourselves when we respect other life on earth.

Leopold also reminds us that "The first order of intelligent tinkering is to save all the pieces." That expression conveys the rationale of wolf restoration and of endangered species recovery programs in general. Recovery programs represent attempts to save pieces as humans tinker, so that future generations will have the opportunity to create a world more complete than the one they inherited.

Several generations of people have seen the wolf obliterated from the land as a result of human tinkering. But equally radical tinkering based on restorative thinking illustrates that pieces can be saved and reassembled in working order, and that restoration is an alternative to extinction.

This illustration is extremely important because, as the world continues to be changed by humankind, increasing numbers of animal and plant species will become endangered as they are squeezed into smaller and smaller "islands" of suitable habitat. Consequently, intensive management programs, such as the one developed for gray wolves in Yellowstone, will be necessary if many species are to persist. And no less than the survival of humankind may depend on this persistence.

During August 1995, I discussed this dependence with President Bill Clinton when he visited the wolf project at Yellowstone. He proffered many opinions on humankind's role as stewards of the earth and suggested that I read the book *The Ecology of Commerce* by Paul Hawken.

Throughout the book, Hawken emphasizes the importance of restoration. He writes, "Exceed sustainability by restoring degraded habitats to their fullest biological capacity. . . . Any viable economic program must turn back the resource clock and devote itself actively to restoring damaged and deteriorating systems. . . . Having expropriated resources from the natural world in order to fuel a rather transient period of materialistic freedom, we must now restore no small measure of those resources. . . . Leave the world better than you found it, take no more than you need, try not to harm life or the environment, make amends if you do."

Hawken's ideas, unfortunately, have yet to capture the

THOUGHTS FROM THE FIELD: RENEE ASKINS

Renee Askins launched the non-profit organization Wolf Fund in 1986 with a single goal: to see wolves returned to Yellowstone. On March 21, 1995, her successful environmental organization closed its doors when we opened the gate to the Crystal Creek pen.

Every morning I look at a photograph that hangs near my desk. It appears to be black and white, except for the shock of a long trail of red blood that stretches from the lower left corner to the middle of the scene. It is an early winter hillside in Yellowstone where the Beartooth Mountains melt down into the Lamar Valley. Somewhere below this hillside, the Mammoth–Cook City road winds through the valley like a paved stream through paradise. The white slope in the photograph is pocked by clumps of sage and an occasional sapling. The faint trace of animal tracks crosses the snow in the upper right corner of the picture. Probably coyote. From behind the shadowy branches of a fir in the lower left corner of the picture, the path of blood emerges, leading across the white snow, ending in the dark silhouette of two animals, one standing, the other prone. They look joined, and in fact are, bonded by the ancient order of predator and prey: to eat and be eaten, to live and die in the oldest rhythm of the world. The silhouettes are those of a gray wolf feeding on an elk calf he has just killed. Three other wolves, each a different shade of gray, are caught in mid-pose below, one dropping into a scent roll, one slinking off with a hunk of hide, and the last observing the rest. It is a freeze frame of the mythic and mundane. It is black and white in color.

Having only had a year to contemplate the meaning of actually having wolves in Yellowstone—after fourteen years of dreaming what it would be like—my dreaming still spills over the reality of their presence, like drifting snow across black pavement. Instead of pinching myself I look at this photograph every morning. It is one of the few black and white renderings of what it means to have wolves back in Yellowstone. I trust it is real because of the red. I trust its meaning because the red is blood. I have learned after fourteen years of working to bring these wolves back to Yellowstone that nothing real is ever black and white, the meaning is always nestled, like a sleeping wolf in the wind-swept snow, somewhere in the shades that drift between black and white.

We are a nation that longs for things to be black and white. We do not like ambiguity. We do not like the uncertain, the unpredictable, the uncontrollable, we like secure borders, we like either/or, all or nothing, black or white, not gray. Wolves come in many shades of gray. In this photograph, their colors range from charcoal to ash, the same colors we see as our world turns from dark to dawn—the crepuscular colors. Wolves travel in those shadows between night and day, between the cultivated and wild, between man and beast, between black and white. It is in this "gray area" that dreams find their home. We mostly know or see wolves in our dreaming, and wolves speak back to our dreaming in the ephemeral way they reveal themselves. A dark, long-legged form floating along the ridge of a steaming geyser basin. Was it? Maybe not. Maybe so. The rising and fading notes of a howl that come and retreat like a tide, leaving its listener wondering. A wolf howl? Yes. No? There was a howl wasn't there? The mirage-like glimmer of a pack through a spotting scope, ten visible, and a split second later, none. It was ten, right? Maybe eight. They were wolves weren't they? Wolves play in our dreams . . . and with our dreams. We sleep better and dream deeper knowing there is a little wildness nuzzling at our door.

It is no surprise that it was the dreaming of a nation, the sheer force of vision and will that bubbled up underneath the veneer of order and dominion, that resulted in the return of wolves to our oldest national park. Wolves slipped into Yellowstone through the cracks in our control and consciousness. Through our dreams, the wolves invite us to follow them through those same cracks, away from the rigidity of dichotomy into the confluence of possibility. We need not decide between black and white, the wild or civilized, the bad or good, the innocent or corrupted. Wolves lead us to the bridges over the chasms of either/or. They can teach us the virtue of our vices and the vices in our virtue. They remind us that the imperfect is our paradise. A fallen tree, a stream stone traverse, a daring leap—we need only follow them, for it is we, not they, who have forgotten how to navigate the nature of the "gray areas." We are of that nature, not apart from it. We survive because of it, not instead of it. Wolves remind us that we find life, take life, and live life neither in the barren black forest nor on the flawless white plain, but, rather, the tracked gray hillside where dark blood weeps into white snow and leaves a trail of red.

Above: **Mike Phillips, Doug Smith, and President Bill Clinton**
*President Bill Clinton and the First Lady visited the Rose Creek
pen to witness first-hand the historic wolf reintroduction.
The Clintons came to Yellowstone just prior to the release of
#9 and her pups.*

Right: **Yellowstone wolf bounding through snow**
According to a Russian proverb, "a wolf is kept fed by its feet."

*Of all the native biological constituents of a
northern wilderness scene, I should say that
the wolves present the greatest test of human
wisdom and good intentions.*
—Paul Errington, Of Predation and Life, 1967

attention of our country. Restoration remains a novel concept about which we know little. Fortunately, the Yellowstone wolf project highlights many of the varied aspects of restoration and, thus, is a logical exemplar for many restoration activities around the world. Good examples always facilitate the learning of a new lesson.

Because humankind exists from a base of finite, non-renewable resources that are being depleted at alarming rates, restoration is critical to maintaining life as we know it. We must begin the age of restoration immedi-

ately, with a devotion so complete that future generations think of restoration as commonplace, a simple fact of life. Wolves in Yellowstone are an important first thread in the national fabric of restorative thinking.

By every measure the Yellowstone wolf restoration project has been successful and has generated benefits that extend beyond the immediate preservation of the species, to positively affect local citizens and communities, larger conservation efforts, and other imperiled species.

For their farsightedness, we commend Americans who support the restoration effort. Additionally, we thank individuals who carefully scrutinize and criticize the project. Their skepticism and questions help identify problems that, once corrected, strengthen the project.

Despite all that wolf restoration is, I can't fathom the complete significance of the program. It's too early. That same conclusion was reached by Park Historian Paul Schullery, who, on the day the wolves were released wrote in a National Park Service memo, "Maybe 120 years from now, Yellowstone managers will be able to look back on this project and make some meaningful judgments on the ecological and spiritual consequences of what we've done today. For the moment, all we can do is give ourselves a little credit for having the belated decency to right such a long-standing wrong and pray for puppies."

And more dreams.

THOUGHTS FROM THE FIELD: NORMAN BISHOP

Norman Bishop is the resources interpreter for the Yellowstone Center for Resources. He has interpreted natural history for thirty-four years in national parks nationwide, but has focused on wolf education at Yellowstone for the last decade.

My most memorable experience related to the Yellowstone wolf project may not have happened yet, but there have been numerous memorable moments.

I'll never forget the thousands of calls and letters I have responded to in the last decade from young people and educators excited about wolves and eager to learn more about them—memorable, and most rewarding. Their letters, expressing thanks and enthusiasm, keep rolling in. Those, and a couple of awards for educating people about wolves, have been gratifying, as has been the appreciation expressed by my colleagues.

The year 1995 has been one long high for me: sort of an emotional ridge walk. January 12 was a good day, when I helped carry the wolves to the Crystal Bench and Rose Creek pens. March 31 was an even better day, when the Crystal Bench pen was opened to release the wolves. Maybe it was January 24 when I nearly choked up; it was then it dawned on me that I was giving my wolf talk for the first time since the wolves were back. I was no longer talking about a proposal to restore wolves. I was relating the story of an active project! About May 1, it was good to hear Joe Fontaine had found eight pups near Red Lodge, after their father had been killed. It was also good to know the pups were returned to Rose Creek to mature safely.

May 13, my wife, Dorothy, and I watched wolves of the Crystal Bench group frolic and run on a distant snowbank. Another day, we watched them work their way west along the trees on the south side of Lamar Valley, opposite the picnic area, moving a few elk and a handful of bison as they went. One of them picked up a piece of hide, and flung it around like a Frisbee. On May 20, we watched the Crystal Bench wolves rally, all with tails wagging, then head uphill quickly to sort out two elk calves and kill them. The elk cows kept chasing the wolves for an hour or more. An amateur from Jackson got video of the whole event, and was generous enough to share a copy of his tape with me.

Cinematographer Bob Landis pursues the wolves tenaciously, patrolling the road through Lamar Valley almost daily, dawn and dusk. His images of the wolves in motion, playing with each other, chasing coyotes, testing and killing elk, and being chased by bison, reinforce my memory of those scenes every time I share them.

Returning October 15 from an overnight stay in upper Slough Creek to the lower meadow to find hundreds of wolf tracks in the snow was memorable. That was the first time I had seen clear wolf tracks in the wild in Yellowstone. That was what I'd been waiting to see.

Now, when I hear a wolf howl some cold, quiet night, or come face to face with an uncollared wolf out there somewhere, I will tell you what was my most memorable experience.

SUGGESTED READINGS

For readers who would like to learn more about wolves, their behavior, and history, the following books are excellent resources:

Bass, Rick. *The Ninemile Wolves*. Livingston, MT: Clark City Press, 1992.

Busch, Robert H. *The Wolf Almanac: A Celebration of Wolves and Their World*. New York: Lyons & Burford, 1995.

Cook, R. S. "Ecological Issues on Reintroduction of Wolves Into Yellowstone National Park." Scientific Monograph NPS\NRYELL\NRSM-93-22. U.S. Department of the Interior, 1993.

Fischer, Hank. *Wolf Wars: The Remarkable Inside Story of the Restoration of Wolves to Yellowstone*. Helena, MT: Falcon Press, 1995.

Link, Mike, and Crowley, Kate. *Following the Pack: The World of Wolf Research*. Stillwater, MN: Voyageur Press, 1994.

Lopez, Barry Holstun. *Of Wolves and Men*. New York: Charles Scribner's Sons, 1978.

McIntyre, Rick. *A Society of Wolves: National Parks and the Battle Over the Wolf, Revised Edition*. Stillwater, MN: Voyageur Press, 1996.

McIntyre, Rick. *War Against the Wolf: America's Campaign to Exterminate the Wolf*. Stillwater, MN: Voyageur Press, 1995.

Mech, L. David. *The Way of the Wolf*. Stillwater, MN: Voyageur Press, 1991.

Mech, L. David. *The Wolf: Ecology and Behavior of an Endangered Species*. Minneapolis: University of Minnesota Press, 1970.

Milstein, Michael. *Wolf: Return To Yellowstone*. Billings, MT: The Billings Gazette, 1995.

Peterson, Rolf O. *The Wolves of Isle Royale: A Broken Balance*. Minocqua, WI: Willow Creek Press, 1995.

Phillips, M. K., and Smith, D. W. "An Administrative History of the Yellowstone Wolf Restoration Program." National Park Service Document, 1996.

Varley, John, and Schullery, Paul. "Reality and Opportunity in the Yellowstone Fires of 1988." In *The Greater Yellowstone Ecosystem: Redefining America's Wilderness Heritage*. New Haven, CT: Yale University Press, 1991.

INDEX

Abbey, Edward, *73*

Absaroka-Beartooth Wilderness, *77, 79*

Acclimation, *26, 55–61, 78*
philosophy, *26, 58*

Alaska Department of Fish & Game, *37*

Alberta, *34, 35, 36*
wolves, *45*

Alberta Fish and Game, *35*

Alligator River Project, *96*

Alpha animals, *46, 50, 60, 69, 72*

American Farm Bureau Federation, *21, 41, 45, 48*

Anderson, Carol, *3*

Animal Damage Control Program (ADC), *3, 107*

Askins, Renee, *3, 8, 121*

Babbitt, Bruce (U.S. Interior Secretary), *16, 21, 41, 42, 49, 52, 63, 83*

Bangs, Ed, *3, 37, 41*

Barbee, Bob, *7, 31*

Baucus, Max, *110*

Bears, *90, 117*

Beattie, Mollie, *41, 42, 49, 52, 63*

Births, wolf, *50–51*

Bishop, Norman, *3, 124*

Black wolf, *45, 98, 116, see also* Wolf, #3
wolves; Wolf, #3

Blacktail Pack, *46, 48–49*

Blacktail pen, *4, 47, 49, 57, 72*

Blackwell, Bob, *3, 55*

Bowers, Al, *58*

Brailsford, Horus and Susan, *107, 110, 111*

Breeding behavior, *46, 60*

Brewster, Wayne, *3, 81, 105*

British Columbia, *34, 36, 42*
wolves, *42, 45, 48*

Buffalo, *22*

Burns, Conrad, *110*

Call of the Wild Foundation, *7, 9, 128*

Capture, *33–37*
philosophy, *34*
1995 operation, *34, 37*
1996 operation, *34, 37*

Caras, Roger, *89*

Care of captive wolves, *58, 60, 71*

Clinton, Bill, *120, 122*

Comfort zone, *62, 66, 69*

Coyotes, *15, 20, 60, 87, 89–90*

Crabtree, Bob, *90*

Crisler, Lois, *51*

Crystal Creek, *46, 66*

Crystal Creek Pack, *46, 65, 66–69, 71, 76–80, 90, 109*
Crystal Creek wolves map, 80

Crystal Creek pen, *28, 29, 45, 47, 55, 66–69, 81*

Cunningham, Ben, *3, 42, 54*

Custer National Forest, *77*

Deaths of wolves, *13, 80, 93, 96*

Defenders of Wildlife, *3, 20, 21, 29, 31, 37, 112*
livestock loss compensation, *3, 20, 29*

Dekker, Dick, *45*

Den sites, *96*

Depredation, *107*

Diet, *44, 55, 58, 60*

Downes, Judge, *21, 45*

Dry Creek Drainage, *107*

Dry Creek incident, *106–115*

Ear tag, *37, 71*

Einstein, Albert, *117*

Elk, *20, 29, 34, 57, 58, 85, 86, 88, 89, 90, 118*

Endangered Species Act, *20, 28–29, 48, 119–120*
delisting of wolves, *29*
experimental-nonessential classification, *28, 29*
history, *28–29*

Environmental Impact Statement (EIS), *16, 21, 39, 41*

Errington, Paul, *122*

Espy, Mike, *16, 21*

Evanoff, Jim, *42, 49*

Feeding, *44, 55, 58, 60*

Finley, Michael, *3, 42, 49, 63*

Fischer, Hank, *3, 7, 8, 21, 31, 125*

Fontaine, Joe, *3, 37, 92, 93, 94, 97*

Fox, *34, 60*

Frazier, Scott, *71*

Fritts, Steve, *3, 37, 43, 66, 67*

Goldman, E. H., *23*

Grand Teton National Park, *28*

Gray wolf, *20, 27, 45*

Ground tracking, *see* Radio tracking, ground

Halfway Pack, *49*

Hard release, *27, 56, 58, 78*
philosophy, *27*
success in Idaho, *56, 78*

Harvey, Paul, *66*

Hawken, Paul, *120*

Hayden Valley, *17*

Helicopter darting, *36*

Homing tendency, *77*

Hoover, Jim, *107, 112*

Howling, *51, 60*

Idaho wolf packs, *77*

Idaho Wolf Restoration, *21*

Inafuku, Les, *3*

Immobilizing drugs, *101, 106*

Incident Command System (ICS), *27*

Injunctions against wolf release, *21, 41, 45, 52*

Jasper National Park, *20*

Jeffers, Robinson, *118*

Johnson, Brian, *68*

Johnson, Mark, *3, 37, 58, 71, 94, 96, 101*

Karle, Marsha, *3, 39*

Kawishiwi Field Lab, *33*

Kennedy, John F., *36*

Kennels, *34, 36–37, 38, 40*

Kills by wolves, *85–91*

Lacey Act, *15*

Lamar River, *57, 75*

Lamar Valley, *80, 85, 86*

Land use patterns, *28, 29*

Landis, Bob, *70, 75, 124*

Leopold, Aldo, *4, 7, 20, 23, 93, 120*

Leopold, Starker, *15*

Lincoln, Abraham, *104*

Livestock, *25, 29*
loss compensation, *25*
losses, *25*

Lopez, Barry, *81, 118, 125*

Lower Falls, *74*

MacKay, Dwight, *110*

Mammoth Hot Springs, Wyoming, *17*

Management zoning, *112*

McClure, Jim, *20, 21*

McKittrick, Chad, *13, 77, 94*

McLeod Pack, *46, 48*

McNey, Mark, *37, 46*

Mech, L. David, *3, 20, 31, 33, 37, 69, 71, 108, 115, 125, 128*

Michigan wolf packs, *58, 77–78*

Minnesota wolf packs, *58, 77*

Montana wolf packs, *29, 30, 56*

Moose, *34, 117, 118*

Mortality mode, *77*

Mott, William Penn, *7, 8, 20, 29, 31*

Mules, *54, 55*

National Park Service, *15, 20, 29, 58*

Neck snares, *36*

Netting, *101*

New Mexico wolf packs, *58*

Nez Perce Pack, *37, 46, 53*

Nez Perce pen, *37, 47, 49, 89*

Niemeyer, Carter, *3, 35, 37, 94*

Nixon, Richard, *20*

O'Neill, Barry, *9, 10–11, 128*

O'Neill, Teri, *9, 10–11, 128*

Old Faithful, *12*

Operation Wolfstock, *27*

Owens, Wayne, *16, 20, 21*

Paradise Valley, Montana, *80*

Paunovich, Ray, *96*

Peaco, Jim, *102*

Pebble Creek Drainage, *117, 119*

Pens, *45–53, 57–61, 66–70, see also* Blacktail pen; Crystal Creek pen; Nez Perce pen; Rose Creek pen; Soda Butte pen construction, *58, 60–61*
design, *58*

Peterson, Rolf O., *103, 125*
Petit Lake Pack, *46*
Phillips, Michael K., *3, 7, 13–37, 42, 65, 67, 82, 91, 93–123, 125, 128*
Physical characteristics, *45*
  coat color, *45, 47*
  weight, *45, 47*
Pimlott, Douglas, *20, 57*
Potter, John, *72*
Predator-prey relationship, *60, 85–91, 118*
Prophylactic parasite control program, *37, 96*
Pups, *14, 47, 92–94, 97–105, 116*
Radio collars, *33, 36, 37, 76, 101–102*
Radio tracking, *36–37, 65, 5–76, 79, 82*
  aerial, *76, 79*
  ground, *76, 82, 119*
Ranchers, *20, 25–26, 29, 30*
  land use issues, *25, 29*
  livestock loss compensation, *20, 25, 29, 31*
  livestock losses, *25, 29*
  opposition to wolves, *25–26*
Reagan, Ronald, *31*
Red Lodge, Montana, *77, 93– 98*
Red wolf, *26, 58, 110*
Redman, Lessie, *75*
Reintroduction, *16, 20–21, 27, 48, 56, 63*
  controversy, *48*
Release, *56, 65–70, 72*
  post-release behavior, *77–80*
Restoration, *see* Yellowstone National Park, wolf restoration
Rick's pack, *48*
River of No-Return Wilderness, *21, 41*
Robinson, Laird, *37, 41*
Rocky Mountain wolf, *20, 27*
Rocky Mountain Wolf Recovery Program, *41, 43*
  recovery areas map, *27*

Roosevelt Arch, *7, 40, 48*
Roosevelt, Theodore, *15*
Rose Creek, *46*
Rose Creek Pack, *46, 65, 69, 76–77, 84, 94–105*
Rose Creek pen, *45, 47, 48, 65, 81, 100–104*
Rutter, Russell, *57*
Schaeffer, Carrie, *102*
Schullery, Paul, *39, 116, 118, 123, 125*
Scientific studies, *26*
Sheldon, Jenny, *90*
Shipping containers, *32, 37, 45*
Sleigh, mule driven, *37, 42, 54, 55*
Slough Creek, *77*
Smith, Douglas W., *3, 7, 45–90, 91, 101, 102, 103, 111–112, 122, 125, 128*
Soda Butte, *69, 78*
Soda Butte Pack, *70, 75–80, 91, 107, 110*
Soda Butte pen, *47, 48, 60, 70*
Soft release, *26, 58*
  philosophy, *26*
  sites, *58*
Specimen Ridge, *68–69*
Stevenson, Donald, *16, 18*
Supporters, wolf, *21, 72*
Taylor, Ken, *37*
Telemetry equipment, *119*
Thoreau, Henry David, *120*
Trackers, *37*
Tracks, *68, 70*
Translocation, *26, 37–43, 47–49, 56*
  map, *42*
  translocation rosters, *47*
  1995 operation, *37, 42, 46, 47*
  1996 operation, *37, 42, 46, 47, 49*
Transplant programs, *34*
Transport kennels, *42, 46*
Trappers, *33, 35*
Turner, John, *43*
U.S. Army, *14–15*
  and Yellowstone, *14–15*
  killing of predators, *14–15*

U.S. Congress, *20, 21*
  conservation laws, *20, 21*
  Endangered Species Act, wolf restoration, *20, 21*
  see also Endangered Species Act
U.S. Customs, *83*
U.S. Department of Interior, *16, 125, see also* Bruce Babbitt
U.S. Department of Justice, *52*
U.S. Fish and Wildlife Service, *3, 20, 21, 29, 36, 120*
U.S. Forest Service, *28*
Vaccinations, *71, 95*
Varley, John, *7–8, 31, 43, 83, 118, 125*
Watt, James, *31*
Weaver, John, *16, 20, 41*
Williston Lake, *34*
Wilson, E. O., *16, 120*
Wines, Wally, *3, 42, 55*
Wolf,
  #2, *46, 47, 78–79*
  #3, *24, 46, 47, 62, 80, 106, 115*
  #4, *46, 47, 62, 79*
  #5, *46, 47, 62, 69, 79*
  #7, *46, 47, 70*
  #8, *47, 62, 79–80, 96, 104*
  #9, *6, 37, 46, 47, 50, 60, 65, 70, 79–80, 93–94, 96*
  #10, *13, 18, 47, 48, 50, 64, 65, 69–70, 93–99, 104*
  #12, *47, 80*
  #13, "old blue," *47, 48, 60, 75, 79*
  #14, *47, 75*
  #15, *47, 75*
  #17, *102, 103*
  #21, *6, 103*
  #22, *96*
  #23, *100–101*
  #29, *44, 47*
  #32, *47, 53*
  #35, *4, 47, 48, 62, 72*
  #36, *47, 48*
  #38, *46, 47*
  #39, *1, 47*
Wolf Education & Research

Center, *37*
Wolf Fund, *3, 121*
Wolf packs, *see* Blacktail Pack; Crystal Creek Pack; Nez Perce Pack; Petit Lake Pack; Rick's Pack; Rose Creek Pack; Soda Butte Pack
Wolf Wars, 7, 31, 125
"Wolves and Humans" exhibit, *20, 31*
"Wolves for Yellowstone?" *16, 21, 41, 43, 81*
Woodring, Sam, *14*
Yellowstone Association, *37*
Yellowstone Center for Resources, *8, 81, 83, 124*
Yellowstone ecosystem, *18, 27, 30, 110*
Yellowstone National Park, *13–22*
  arrival of wolves, *40, 45–53*
  conservation, *29*
  greater Yellowstone area map, *28*
  history, *13–16, 20–21*
  killing of predators in, *13, 14–15, 16, 20*
  movements of Yellowstone wolves map, *80*
  release of wolves, *75–83*
  ungulate populations, *22, 30*
  wolf restoration, *16, 20–21, 25–31, 39, 41, 43, 96, 117–123*
Yellowstone River drainage, *110*
Yellowstone Wolf Recovery Fund, *119, 121*
Young, Stanley P., *23, 35*
Zallen, Margot, *41*

ABOUT THE AUTHORS

Michael K. Phillips, left, and Douglas W. Smith, center, watch for wolves with wolf researcher L. David Mech, after the opening of the Soda Butte pens in 1995. (Photo © Barry and Teri O'Neill)

Michael K. Phillips is the project leader for the Yellowstone Gray Wolf Restoration Project. From 1986 to 1994, he was the coordinator of field projects for the red wolf recovery program in the southeastern United States, which successfully restored the red wolf to parts of its former range throughout that region. Phillips is in fact the only person in the world with intimate knowledge of both the Yellowstone gray wolf program and the red wolf project, which are the only two wolf restoration efforts ever attempted. He has worked with noted wolf researcher Dr. L. David Mech and has written numerous magazine and newspaper articles. He has also done research on grizzly and black bears, coyotes, red foxes, and dingoes. He holds a Masters of Science in Wildlife Ecology from the University of Alaska and presently makes his home in Mammoth, Wyoming, with his wife and three children.

Douglas W. Smith is the wolf biologist for the Yellowstone Gray Wolf Restoration Project. He worked extensively with Dr. Rolf O. Peterson in his studies of the wolf-moose relationship on Isle Royale National Park, Michigan, and with other leading wolf biologists, including Dr. L. David Mech in northern Minnesota and Dr. Erich Klinghammer in Indiana. He is presently completing his Ph.D. in Ecology, Evolution, and Conservation Biology at the University of Nevada, Reno, where he also teaches. He has numerous publication credits in both the scientific and popular media. This is his first book.

Barry and Teri O'Neill have over thirty years of combined photography experience and a keen interest in the outdoors and wildlife issues. The O'Neills founded the Call of the Wild Foundation, a nonprofit corporation, to support the restoration of wolves to Yellowstone National Park. The Foundation's mission is to ensure the long-term success of the Yellowstone Gray Wolf Restoration Project by raising funds, providing information, and generating support. The O'Neills were allowed access to the inner workings of the restoration project, and their photographs of the new Yellowstone residents are unique, the only up-close photography of the entire effort.

Barry and Teri O'Neill. (Photo © Tom Torgove)